Weathering Locomotives

Tim Shackleton

Ian Allan
PUBLISHING

Previous page: *Noisy, animated and hot to the touch, the steam engine is the nearest object to a living thing that man has ever invented. A hint of weathering always brings locomotive models to life, and this Hornby 'Castle' illustrates the basic techniques I'll be demonstrating in this book. Taking an otherwise out-of-the-box model, I've gently misted a selection of warm-grey brown tones over areas such as the wheels, motion, running plate, cab roof and tender top, using variations of my standard weathering mix (Revell No 8 Matt Black and Humbrol No 62 Matt Leather). These parts get dirty very quickly on any steam locomotive – just look at* **Tornado** *before and after a main-line run. Airbrush overspray drifts up over the cab and tender sides, helping to knock back the over-bright lining a little. Once the basic weathering was complete, I took some very dilute Metalcote Gunmetal and sprayed it onto the boiler and other green-liveried areas, allowing it to collect by capillary action in the nooks and crannies. Once dry, I polished it with a cotton bud. This gives a wonderful metallic sheen and also simulates the distinct blackening you see on green engines; as the paint ages blues fade, but green darkens appreciably over time. The result is a one-off model of a working locomotive rather than a highly-detailed commercial product identical to several thousand others.* Tony Wright

MIX
Paper from
responsible sources
FSC® C014615
FSC
www.fsc.org

First published 2011

ISBN 978 0 7110 3656 7

Published by Ian Allan Publishing
an imprint of Ian Allan Publishing, Ltd, Hersham, Surrey KT12 4RG.
Printed in England by Ian Allan Printing Ltd, Hersham, Surrey KT12 4RG.

Visit the Ian Allan Publishing website at www.ianallanpublishing.com

Distributed in the United States of America and Canada by BookMasters Distribution Services.

CONTENTS

Pristine newness is exceptional in real railway practice, but seems to be very prevalent in models, and though British railways have had a very chequered career of rebuilding and modification for more than a hundred years, things really new and spotlessly clean are extremely rare.

Rust-stained water tanks, broken engine-shed windows and the modest accumulation of rubbish at the foot of embankments all go to make the 'age' effect apparent to the onlooker, who will secretly admire the realism so achieved. Such ageing, though it is guaranteed to improve any model layout, must only be carried into effect with constant consultation with the 'real thing', otherwise the overall effect might be made rather bizarre, or even absurd. An hour spent on a station will give more ideas in this respect than many pages of cautions and descriptions.

Ernest F. Carter, *The Model Railway Encyclopaedia*
(*Burke Publishing, London, 1950*)

Acknowledgements

A fair number of friends have helped – sometimes inadvertently – to put this book together. I'd like to thank the following modellers in particular for their support, encouragement, good advice and constructive criticism: Arran Aird; Chris Gibbon; Pete Hill; Roy Jackson; Geoff Kent; Chris Langdon; Roy C. Link; Barry Norman; Chris Pendlenton; Mick Simpson; Tony Sissons; John Sutton; Chris Walsh; Tim Watson; Alan Whitehouse; Vincent Worthington; Tony Wright. My gratitude also goes out to the always enthusiastic and ambitious students I have taught (and who have sometimes taught me) on my residential courses at Hobby Holidays and at Missenden Abbey.

All photographs were taken by the author except where noted.

Backtracking

Effective weathering is one of the key factors in encouraging your trains to blend in with the modelled landscape. A 50-year-old building doesn't look like it was put up yesterday, so why should a 50-year-old locomotive resemble a toy straight out of the box? Trackwork, civil engineering, lineside structures and the trains themselves should all look comfortable and of a piece with one another. With this in mind, the Manchester Model Railway Society's 00 gauge layout Dewsbury Midland is one of the best integrated models I know. The consistent way everything is painted makes as much an impact as the across-the-board quality of the modelling. This is the naturalistic school at its best, all the more effective for its wholly urban context and for being very much a club effort created by different hands and – just as significantly – different pairs of eyes. The fact that the layout setting is very much the part of the world I come from makes it ring even more true for me.

One advantage of being as old as I am is that you can see how patterns have developed in your life. It applies on a large scale – the places you live and work, the people you live and work with – and on a very small scale too. Railway modelling – like girls, photography and Rugby League – has been a lifelong interest for me and I can chart my existence on this planet by recalling what (or who) I was making, photographing or watching at any given moment.

Since most of my railway models still survive – give or take the odd Airfix mineral wagon that finally disintegrated into its constituent parts – I can see how far I have progressed (or not) in the intervening years. For much of that time, the way the models were painted has been at least as important to me as their construction. I have always been very self-critical and I can remember, when I was ten or 11, comparing my Kitmaster 'Duchess' with the identical model built by a school friend. His was much better made – no residual sprue tags or glue marks to spoil the effect – but the way mine was painted gave it a distinct edge, in my mind if in no one else's.

In subsequent years (of which there have been many), I've needed to devote far more effort to improving my constructional skills than I have to paintwork, which has always come naturally to me. When I was 13 years old, I realised there was a whole new dimension to this subject. It wasn't enough to simply paint a model in a colour approximating LMS maroon, Deltic blue or freight-stock bauxite – some attempt had to be made to bestow an element of realism upon it, simulating the effects of wind, rain, smoke, steam, dirt or general decrepitude. Weathering models began for me – as I expect it did for many of my generation – with a Terence Cuneo article in a small book published by Rovex entitled *Tri-ang Railways: The First 10 Years*. It was a seminal piece in which he described how, by using artists' oil paint, he'd turned a small, blue and very plasticky tank engine called *Nellie* into something approximating a model of a hard-working locomotive.

Seeing Cuneo's *Nellie* was a moment of pure revelation. A month or two earlier I'd been admiring pictures of beautifully weathered American locomotives in the pages of *Model Railway News*, but I had absolutely no idea of how to achieve such effects. Cuneo was the one who showed me how it could be done and, because I'd always liked the gritty sense of realism evident in his work (even in my pre-teen years), I accepted his authority without question. I don't think he ever had much interest in model railways, despite a fair number of his paintings being used as covers for Tri-ang catalogues, but that didn't stop him applying his vision and technical skills to model trains.

How long has weathering been around?

John Allen may not have invented weathering – a term that, in a modelling context, first appears in print in the December 1939 issue of *Model Railroader* – but in the late 1940s and throughout the 1950s he was certainly its most influential and innovative proponent. His HO scale Gorre & Daphetid Railroad was to American finescale modelling what John Ahern's Madder Valley or Peter Denny's Buckingham Branch were to the UK, only on a far larger scale.

Ahern and Denny applied a little gentle weathering to their track and lineside structures, but Allen went several steps further and treated everything – including the locomotives and stock. The earliest UK article by John Allen I can find is in the *Model Railway News* for March 1948 – a two-page piece on his original 6ft 8in by 3ft 7in Gorre & Daphetid layout, then under construction. Although the post-war paper and print quality is very poor, one of the photos shows a well-weathered dockside saddle tank with a rake of rust-pocked bogie ore hoppers.

Allen was a regular contributor to *Model Railroader* and, as a professional photographer, also produced advertising stills for the kit manufacturer Varney. These often featured locomotives that had been built – and weathered – by Allen, although readers had to wait until the December 1955 and January 1956 issues to find out how he did it. He suggests a mixture of Floquil black, white and boxcar red worked into a warm grey; the firebox, smokebox and areas below the boiler plumbing should be streaked with a lighter tone:

> *I prefer to weather locos with flat oils or lacquer, even if the loco is already painted flat black . . . Locos are handled more than cars and need more permanent paint. If you wish to dirty a painted loco, cover the surface with a thinned-down wash of gray [that will] allow much of the original black to show through. Let it streak in the directions water would normally flow. Let the smokebox, firebox and possibly the cylinders be a lighter gray. These parts burn off first.*
>
> *Wherever there is steam leakage such as at safety valves, whistle or air pump, a grey-white substance will cover the surface and wash down unless it is regularly cleaned off. A little light grey flat paint put on thinly will simulate these stains.*
>
> *I give unpainted locomotives a covering coat of black mixed with white, and a touch of brown to make a warm gray. I brush it on, stroking in the directions water would run. I occasionally dip my brush into black, white or brown paint and streak it down the locomotive side to simulate a patch of soot, boiler compound or rust . . .*

As far as I'm aware, this is the first practical guidance on weathering ever published. Andrew Emmerson – finescale historian emeritus – has a collection of model railway textbooks from the USA, France, Germany and Holland going back to the 1930s which contain nothing about weathering. British modellers seem to have been equally slow to catch onto Allen's lead, though Peter Denny (and possibly others) spoke approvingly of the effect that repeated handling had in toning paintwork down to a more naturalistic appearance.

All the same, there were glimmerings. Peco produced 'weathered' versions of their Wonderful Wagons in the 1950s with replacement planks, etc. In the October 1955 *Railway Modeller* there was a piece on building an ERG cattle wagon kit – how the author achieved the limewashing effect on the planked sides is not mentioned. As far as RTR manufacturers are concerned, Roy C. Link reminds us that, as the 1950s went on, there was a steady move away from 'glossy' finishes to more plausible satin/matt combinations – particularly on goods locomotives.

As the 1960s dawned there were vague hints in UK magazines about weathering freight stock with washes of dirty thinners, but I can find no sign of a weathered locomotive until Terence Cuneo's article on weathering *Nellie* appeared in the handbook *Tri-ang Railways – The First 10 Years* (though the publication date is given as 1962, the book did not actually appear until 1963). In the May 1963 *Model Railway News* there were photos of weathered S-scale US locomotives – as a 12-year-old, this was the first proper weathering I'd ever seen.

At the same time, Bob Essery began his hugely influential *Railway Modeller* series on building 4mm wagons. Most were weathered by Arthur Whitehead, newly returned from Canada where he had been closely involved with the local model railroading scene and would undoubtedly have encountered the Allen-esque techniques he described in the *Railway Modeller* articles. This was the first time, Bob tells me, that he can recall seeing weathered models. While other UK modellers also point to the early sixties as the starting point, it was still very episodic – a locomotive here, a building there – and some prominent figures (David Jenkinson, for one) shunned weathering completely. On the whole it was very far removed from the integrated approach we see nowadays, as Iain Rice remembers:

Top right: John Allen's Gorre & Daphetid c1952, from a contemporary advertisement.

Below: The model that inspired a new generation of weatherers: Terence Cuneo's stunning rendition of **Nellie** in artist's oils and turps came complete with instructions on how to achieve similar effects.

The first layout I can recall featuring overall weathering – locos included – was the West Lancs O Gauge group's LMS layout Diggle and Halebarns, which was prominent in the hobby in the early 1970s. Ken Longbottom was the moving spirit. It was 0 fine scale (not very fine finescale!), L & Y themed, situated in several sheds in a large garden, linked by 'box tunelled' track. It was predominantly an operating layout, fully signalled. Most of the modelling was a bit crude but it certainly had atmosphere – the whole thing was very gritty, a sort of Brief Encounter *in 7mm scale! It made a nice antidote to the brand of sanitised finescale modelling that was around at the time.*

Right: A grubby-
looking King's Courier
speeds through the
altogether cleaner
and more agreeable
landscape on Tony
Wright's layout,
Little Bytham. A dirty
engine on a prestige
express was an
all-too-common sight
in the final years of
steam. I weathered
the 'A1' according to
Tony's specification at
a Missenden Abbey
railway modeller's
weekend. This section
of the layout was still
very much a work in
progress when this
picture was taken.
The platforms are little
more than sketches,
but how much
better those Hornby
Pullmans look with
a good bit of sooting
on the roofs! This is
the fourth complete
Pullman rake I've
weathered – two for
Tony, and another two
for Roy Jackson – and
only one car out of 30-
odd I've painted is still
in ex-works condition.
I only touch the roofs,
ends and underframe,
generally preferring to
give the sides only the
very faintest toning-
down. Tony Wright

I can honestly say the Cuneo article changed my life. Armed with a copy and a selection of oils left over from a painting-by-numbers set, I got down to work. The first model I weathered was an elderly Tri-ang 'Jinty' borrowed from another school friend. I 'super-detailed' it for him, which meant adding some crushed coal to the bunker and a couple of crew figures, and renumbered it (by hand) to 47300 – that it had to be a Spital Bridge engine had a significance now lost to me. Its shiny Margate black was soon buried under assorted shades of browns and greys; I liked the effect, though the owner wasn't so sure.

Next up was my three-rail stuff. The oil paints had taken an aeon to dry and so, not yet having learned the merits of patience, I switched to Humbrol enamels. I think my '8F' came first, then the BR 2-6-4T and the *Duchess of Montrose* (which later, horror of horrors, acquired a coat of BR blue). Because Cuneo had shown me such things, I was well into epic displays of limescaling and burned smokebox doors, without thinking for a moment about whether such touches were appropriate to my models. (They were not – at least for a layout supposedly located somewhere in the Shrewsbury area in order to justify the coexistence of a 'Duchess' and a 'Castle'.) Everything was done by brush, of course, and I don't think I bothered thinning the paint. The weathering shades were painted straight on, a livery of spectacular drabness.

Pretty soon, however, I realised that real locomotives and rolling stock weathered differently, and not always as prescribed by Cuneo. Although I bought the *Railway Modeller* every month and occasionally saw *Model Railway*

Right: Weathered
S-scale 0-6-0
switcher by Jim
Konas, from the May
1963 Model Railway
News.

Inspired by Terence Cuneo, this Hornby-Dublo '8F' is one of the first locomotives I ever weathered, c1963, using artist's oils. The finish is a little battered after almost half a century but all the essentials are there – the build-up of rust and brake-block dust below the footplate, the limescaling and even the deposits of emulsified oil thrown out by the cylinders Bear in mind that this wasn't copied from photographs, but directly from the real thing. The number repeated on the tender rear was quite common at the time but I've never seen it on a model. The hybrid LMS/BR livery was suited to a layout supposedly set in 1950, the year I was born.

Constructor, I can't remember seeing much practical advice about weathering. (With the exception in later years of the upmarket *Model Railway Journal* and *Narrow Gauge and Industrial Railway Modelling Review*, weathering has always been sparsely covered in British magazines by comparison with the American modelling press.) So instead of copying other people's models, I studied the prototype instead – an approach that I've followed to this day.

This was around 1963-4, when there was plenty of amazing 12in:foot weathering to be seen on British Railways. A rust-pocked 16T mineral duly appeared and a bulk grain hopper was similarly embellished. My coaching stock acquired darkened roofs and brownish underframes, and I painted my three-rail track to match.

The first examples of weathered locomotives I ever saw were US-outline models. It's therefore appropriate that this magnificent 'Allegheny' 2-6-6-6 has become something of a test-bed for new methods suggested by American friends close to the cutting edge of HO-scale modelling. I think this cross-fertilisation of ideas is healthy, since British weathering techniques are far from identical to those used by US modellers.

I could see that the effects of weathering were an integral part of the real railway scene, which in turn enhanced my appreciation of it. I have no interest whatsoever in the technicalities of locomotive lore and only the very faintest appreciation of railway history. What I enjoy is observing the railway in general and trains in particular. I like listening to it also – from the luxuriously deep and almost subliminal hum of Eurostar to the mechanical thrash of a first-generation DMU and the purposeful, unbelievably evocative flank-flonk-flank-flonk of a WD – especially when heard at night. Best of all, I like seeing the workaday railway going about its familiar routines, with the sense of purpose and unhurried but still highly disciplined manner in which a network operates.

In the steam days I loved the heroic filthiness of sheds like Annesley and Langwith Junction; their never-cleaned '9Fs' and 'O4s' were a mass of lime-streaking and rusting decrepitude – even reading the numbers was difficult in poor light. It seemed somehow so fitting, so much a part of the overall scene. I took to heart a line in Colin Gifford's magisterial *Decline of Steam*: 'A grubby ROD is as appropriate at the head of a coal train as a shining "Deltic" on the "Queen of Scots".' Cuneo may have been the initial inspiration but it was Gifford's visual approach – derived in great part from the work of pioneering Swiss avant-garde railway photographer Jean-Michel Hartmann in the 1950s – that had the biggest overall influence on the way I looked at railways, the way I photographed them, the models I built and how I painted them.

Right: This is where we start – fresh from delivery by Brush, re-engined 57004 *Freightliner Quality* sits in the yard at Ipswich on 23 May 1999. It looks like a new toy straight out of its box – or does it? RTR models as bought tend to have an unconvincingly matt or semi-matt finish, whereas ex-works and freshly-cleaned locomotives are normally very shiny indeed. Quite a bit of work is needed to recreate a gleaming, factory-fresh finish on an as-bought or newly completed model, as we will see. On the other hand, a touch of weathering on a matt-finish RTR locomotive will really bring it to life.

Above: Closer up, we can see this Class 57 is less than pristine – there's a hint of overspill around the sandboxes and clear signs of streaking where rainwater has washed down the sides.

By 1965, however, much of my Dublo empire had been sold off (its trade-in value, already miserable, must have been reduced still further by my weathering efforts) and a pile of Formoway two-rail track appeared. I built a London Midland Region layout (or rather a large through station called 'Winslade') in my bedroom, and while the trackwork and structures were religiously weathered, it never ran. Pretty soon, modelling was parked on the back burner on a very slow simmer. Real, live steam was well on the way out and had to be photographed while there was still time; my match-winning fantasies required acting out on the rugby field; most importantly of all, girls had entered my life.

Fast forward a decade and a half: I'm now divorced, working in publishing and, while I've photographed a lot of industrial steam in the interim, I've done very little modelling – other than building an 'N7' and a few items of stock for a still unbuilt model layout of a Great Eastern branch in BR days. (You'll note the intentionally catholic pattern of my modelling interests, which continues to this day.) Weathering these kit-built, 4mm-scale models was the most interesting part of the operation – I'd mix matt black and track colour in different proportions, thin it slightly and brush it onto the model: a darker warmish grey for the upper works, a brake block-brown colour on the wheels and an oily tan colour on the rods. Almost immediately, I'd dip the brush in thinners (I used turpentine in those days) and take most of the weathering off again, allowing it to collect in corners and out-of-the-way spots that a cleaner's rag could never reach.

This was the way we did things back then and it's still the way a lot of people do it now, even though so many new techniques and technologies are open to us. (John Sutton and Geoff Kent, for instance, can weather a model just as well as I can, yet to them an airbrush is something used for 'brushing your 'air'.)

And then one day, feeling particularly benign after a good lunch – something of a speciality in publishing 30 years ago; it isn't like that now – I saw an Airfix '4F' in the window of Hambling's, that wonderful and much-missed modelling shop just off the Charing Cross Road, where in summer you could listen to the test-match commentary while browsing its extensive stocks of railway books. The '4F' was duly bought for a fiver or so (they were knocking them out dirt-cheap in a factory clearance), renumbered and given a modest level of extra detailing.

Weathering the '4F' was a necessity to my way of thinking. Although I'd never owned anything grander than a few sable brushes, I'd seen and admired the new-fangled airbrushes that were appearing in the better model shops. On an editor's pittance there was no way that I could afford a good one, so I bought a simple hobby spray. I exhausted the can of propellant by practising airbrushing via spraying ink on paper; I got the hang of it pretty quickly, even though my range of options and effects was severely limited. Then it was the '4F's turn. At that time my aesthetic – first evolved in three-rail days and developed through the handful of kits I'd built in intervening years – still favoured dark grey upper works and a brownish tone below the running plate, the two being delicately blended at the division point.

I discovered one fundamental rule almost immediately – that airbrushed paint dries appreciably lighter than it goes on wet, the opposite to most household paints. I'd be spraying away and thinking, 'That section needs a slightly darker tone over the top of it'; so I'd go over it again and then, two minutes later, realise that the whole model was exactly the same colour. At first it requires a considerable leap of imagination to forecast just how a colour is going to turn out, but the ability is acquired very quickly.

From that point on, weathering models (and especially locomotives) became my personal journey of discovery. You may have seen my work in *Model Railway*

Above: On 15 July 2002, 66041 and its rake of 17 brand-new HTAs positively gleam as they negotiate the crossovers at Milford Junction with coal for one of the Aire Valley power stations. It makes for a magnificent sight – but it's a very transient moment in time, hardly typical of the most intensive freight service in the UK. Only the sooting from the locomotive exhaust – always the first part of a locomotive to weather – spoils the image of visual perfection, enhanced by a beautiful summer's day. This is the adman's dreamworld beloved of the monthly railway magazines, and of many modellers too.

Left: Roll forward a year or two and this is what Aire Valley coal looks like as a filthy 66143 makes exactly the same move on 22 December 2006. A hard frost clings to the landscape – it was, after all, the day of the winter solstice. Brake dust coats the GM's nether regions and there's oil spillage from the fuel tank, though there's still a measure of shininess at cantrail level and around the cab front. The wagons, however, bear evidence of round-the-clock operation and the winter rains have washed layers of coal fines down their once-gleaming flanks.

Journal, on my Right Track DVD, *Weathering Techniques*, or at one of the shows where I demonstrate my techniques. You may even have been a student at one of the residential courses I teach. If you have, I think you'll appreciate that there's a strong measure of consistency in my work, but also a willingness to experiment and try out new ideas, always with enhanced realism in mind. Whether or not you've encountered my work before, I hope that you may learn something from the following pages.

It staggers me now to think I've been using an airbrush for close on 30 years (and still can't put on a base livery coat as smooth as those routinely achieved by Ian Rathbone and Chris Wesson). During that time-span there have been diversions, missed turnings and blind alleys galore. For some time, especially when Bernie Victor's shop near King's Cross station was still open, I used imported Floquil and Polly S pre-mixed weathering colours from the USA. The quality of the paint was incredible, but I didn't realise the desert sun does things to a Southern Pacific diesel that don't apply to locomotives working over Stainmore Summit or Ais Gill. Locomotives that I weathered in the late 1980s/early 90s acquired a bleached-bones look that – had I studied my reference photographs more closely – I should have realised wasn't really suited to British prototypes. (This is why I make sure my Humbrol-weathered Espee and Santa Fe power readily translates into something that might be seen in the Mojave Desert or on Cajon Pass.)

Like most modellers, I have many boxes of paint tins acquired over the years – the oldest (still in occasional use) is a can of Humbrol mid-green bought when I was a student, the best part of 40 years ago. Many of these were acquired for weathering purposes, but I used them a few times and moved on because, at an early stage, I'd discovered that most airbrush weathering relies on no more than four colours – any old matt black (a charcoal grey will do just as well), Humbrol matt leather (No 62), Humbrol Metalcote Gunmetal (which is not one and the same as the conventional gunmetal colour, No 53) and occasionally a drop of matt white. If I use anything else, unless it's blended in to the point of invisibility, then it sticks out like a train-spotter at a hen party.

Becoming a regular contributor to (and subsequently editor of) *Model Railway Journal* introduced me to new people and new ideas. Although I primarily thought of myself as a builder of locomotives – either heavily adapted RTR or, in preference, a top-of-the-range etched kit – people started to take more and more notice of my weathering. Martyn Welch was my predecessor at *MRJ* and, during his tenure, we used to have endless conversations about weathering techniques and much else besides. If Martyn took me seriously, I told myself, I had to be onto something. Some years earlier I'd bought his book, *The Art of Weathering*, and was amazed to find how similar our techniques were; in that sense, I learned very little from Martyn's demonstration of his methods, but found much of value in the generous selection of prototype photographs.

The turning point came in around 2002, when I became involved with Roy Jackson's monumental Retford project. In a purpose-built structure deep in RAF bomber country, Roy and friends have made major progress with a gargantuan EM gauge showing Retford on the East Coast main line at the point where it crosses the ex-Great Central Sheffield-Lincoln line. It's roughly 80 x 30ft and fully operational (if only partially scenic as yet), with four huge staging yards containing enough stock to run a fair representation of the 1957 summer timetable with minimum repetition. Given a sunny day and a tail wind, we can work though WTT in five or six hours with a generous break for lunch.

There are something like 90 complete trains on the railway; without fully realising it (Roy is good at subtle persuasion), I somehow undertook to weather as many of them as I could manage to a uniform standard. Getting to the railway is a 300-mile round trip for me; in order to make maximum use of time spent there (and to preserve my sanity and health), I needed to find a way of weathering the locomotives and stock without taking forever and a day. At home, I can happily spend a weekend on a single locomotive, an afternoon on a carriage and an hour or more on a wagon. On a two-day visit to Lincolnshire, I need to be able to finish five or six locomotives, or a couple of 15-coach trains, and to have them back in the fiddle yard (Roy insists that the wheels are thoroughly cleaned) ready for the next running day. I also need to get up to Barnetby to look at some real trains . . .

My solution enabled me to achieve 75 or 80 percent of the effect in half the time or less. Retford is so big that a 50-wagon freight or the 'Flying Scotsman' could easily get lost on its mile-long scenic section; close inspection inevitably takes second place to marvelling at the overall effect. What I came up with was a shorthand approach to weathering, a distillation of four decades of experience into a far more manageable time-span. This is, essentially, what we're going to be looking at in this book.

So how do I go about weathering one of Retford's locomotives? If I can't paint outdoors (which is how I work at home), I'll set up on a small table in the railway room, close to the big sliding doors, so that I'm assured of a constant supply of fresh air. I'll have discussed beforehand exactly what I'll be working on and what effects are required; I'll have been through my library (and Roy's, which is even more extensive) to find suitable photographs for reference and inspiration – a shiny 'B1', a grubby 'A2', whatever is on my painting turntable. I'll have brought

It's a fair bet that, except when brand new, no Ivatt 2-6-0 ever looked remotely like this out-of-the-box Bachmann model. The detail is exquisite and yet the finish is totally plastic. In this state it just doesn't look natural, and yet you can see dozens of locomotives just like this at any exhibition.

Ready-to-run models can look lovely straight out of the box, but that's basically all they are – models. Because their finish is so unworldly, they fail to convince – real locomotives have never looked like this, even when fresh from shops. This 7mm-scale shunting locomotive from DJH is beautifully made and impeccably finished – it runs very nicely too – but to my mind it just cries out for the subtle weathering that will ultimately bring it to life.

Right: *An Ivatt
as it should be –
Chris Pendlenton's
wonderfully
naturalistic depiction
of No 43126 (the
Bachmann model
extensively reworked
to P4 standards
with Brassmasters
underpinnings and
other refinements),
sitting in the shed
yard on Chris's
equally convincing
model of early 1960s
North Shields. The
layout's location is
entirely fictional and
yet all the elements
of a long-vanished
Tyneside are captured
to perfection.
Everything is in
harmony – the sooty
ex-North Eastern
signal, the battered
yard lamp, the piles
of ash, the oily
motionwork on the
locomotive.*
Chris Pendlenton

with me a choice of airbrushes, a compressor, an extension lead, paint, thinners, weathering powders, paintbrushes, something to release the tops of paint cans (the handle of my best tweezers usually), other items listed in the 'Equipment' section and lots of kitchen roll, to deal with the inevitable spills and mess.

Once I'm set up, I'll prop my pictures up in front of me – out of spraying range – and simply get on with it. 'Just do it!' has become a kind of Retford mantra. As a loosely knit group, we prefer to crack on with things rather than sit around agonising over the finer points of modelling (or 'fannying around', to use Mr Jackson's preferred term). The fact that, so far in his modelling lifetime, Roy and friends have built five very large working layouts (Gainsborough Central, Ancaster, High Dyke, Dunwich and now Retford) suggests there is some validity to this approach.

**Right and
below:** *Another
transformation, this
time of a Bachmann
BR Standard
Class 5. Cosmetic
enhancement
has largely been
restricted to buffer-
beam fittings and
firebox pipework but
I put a lot of effort
into the weathering,
trying to match a
schoolboy snap of
No 73164 simmering
outside Mirfield
shed one August
evening in 1962.
Even Martyn Welch
was impressed with
this one!*

So what you see in the step-by-step sequences that form the core of this book is exactly what happens at Roy's place, or in my own garden at home. There's no great mystique to it – although there may be a certain kind of alchemy that I've grown familiar with. I will look at matters such as equipment and technique, and the all-important business of looking at your prototype. And of course observation is the key to successful weathering, far more so than anything that you can buy or learn to use. My approach to weathering is a very personal one that has evolved over time, but it is by no means unique. Indeed, I'm told by another Roy – Roy C. Link, doyen of narrow-gauge modellers and one of the finest graphic designers I've ever worked with – that mine is a very English technique, involving as it does a lot of airbrushing and endless cans of enamel paint.

(Americans, for instance, do things very differently – far less airbrush, a lot more drybrush, much hand-finishing, oodles of time-intensive dustings and washings that call for infinite patience. The really top guys, such as Rodney Walker, Jim Six or the legendary Hummer Dave, can spend anything up to six months weathering a single model. This is not a luxury I can afford.)

Above: A decent weathering job can turn a less-than-perfect base model into something seriously convincing. By comparison with what would come later from Bachmann and ViTrains, the Lima Class 37 was badly flawed in some areas – especially the nonexistent bodyside turnunder – but it was still a good starting point and, like many Lima models, it had delicacy of detail.

Left: Even with careful weathering, some models are beyond redemption. This is the old Tri-ang version of Evening Star *as subsequently relaunched, 40 years on, as part of Hornby's budget-priced Railroad range. I gave it a ten-minute weathering as part of a Missenden Abbey tutorial but its failings are still obvious.*
Tony Wright

Right: It's easy to overcook weathering effects and reduce them to parody, with decrepit rustbucket locomotives operating in indescribably filthy conditions. It's true that this is how it sometimes was (Polkemmet Colliery comes to mind), but I think Steffan Lewis has got it just about right in his P4 model of Maindee East engine shed. There never was a Maindee East, of course, but this model of an ex-Great Western 'Loan Act' shed in its final days captures the rain-washed character of the South Wales valleys with sensitivity and understatement.

Left: You should always try and make sure the finish on your locomotives matches their working environment. The 10-strong clutch of 204bhp Andrew Barclay 0-6-0DMs – unique to the Eastern Region – came from a pure industrial design and spent their working lives out of the public gaze at places such as Boston docks and Staveley ironworks. My P4 model of D2403 – note the oil seepage on the body-side doors and the sheen of spilled fuel on the tank – was built from a Judith Edge kit and is seen in an appropriately industrial setting. The buildings are predominantly made of card, one of my favourite modelling materials, with corrugated cladding from styrene sheets.

At the same time my approach, while consistent, is far from standardised, as you'll see in the 'Portfolio' chapter, which shows a variety of diversely weathered models – each of them, I hope, subtly different. Inevitably, 4mm scale will predominate because it's the one I mostly work in, but the same methods are applicable to other scales. In fact, the scale is not particularly critical when talking about weathering techniques. In recent years I have weathered models in quite a variety of scales, from 2mm to 7mm and beyond, and the techniques are much the same. The bigger the model, the better the airbrush appears to be working.

There are, of course, further ways of enhancing realism – this is not strictly about weathering but about bringing a model to life through small creative touches, once again based on observation: tender water fillers with the lids left open; scuff marks on cab doors; half-open cab windows; firemen leaning nonchalantly out of the cab; choosing the right kind of coal for the job (nice big lumps for an express engine, dusty rubbish for a shunting locomotive) and considering how it is stacked in the tender; unofficially customised numberplates and smokebox door hinges; patch-painted repairs; grubby weathersheets; authentic-looking dings and dents; nicely bent pipework; chalk markings and the like – even graffiti. Most people don't notice these things but are amazed when they see them on a model. None of these embellishments costs much (if anything) to put into practice – it's all about having an eye for the way things are and studiously observing the real thing.

So let's crack on, shall we?

Above: *If we model any period earlier than the 1970s, we tend to look to black and white photographs for reference and inspiration. My impression of pre-nationalisation railways is purely monochrome – I don't think of them in colour at all and I find colour photographs of the railways of that period vaguely disconcerting. It's possible, with experience, to learn how to interpret b/w images for information about weathering but I find it helpful, once in a while, to reverse the process and photograph my steam-era models in monochrome just to check that I'm still on course and that my locomotives accurately reflect the prototype and mirror what's seen in contemporary images. This BR Standard Class 4 2-6-4T is a Bachmann model converted to P4 – behind the cosmetic sideframes (Comet etches) the chassis block is the original but the sprung bogie and pony truck are new. The bodywork carries a lot of extra detail to reflect the differences evident on different batches – in this instance, one of the early Southern Region examples. The weathering was derived from a mixture of colour and b/w photographs.*

Below and Bottom: *Roy Jackson likes to see clean Pacifics on Retford, but that's not to say they can't benefit from a fair bit of weathering – especially below the running plate. Otherwise, these Hornby Pacifics are virtually untouched apart from renumbering and conversion to EM gauge.*

CHAPTER

Portfolio

As a magazine editor, it has always annoyed me that the average loco-building article devotes about 50 words to how the model was weathered and about 5000 to how it was built. I for one would like to know a little more than 'The final stage was to weather the locomotive, using Humbrol enamels,' or worse – 'I sent the model to a professional to be weathered.'

If this kind of thing leaves me none the wiser – a man who has spent almost 50 years weathering railway models – then I don't know what good it can be doing anyone else. It's on the same level as saying, 'The inside motion fell together one afternoon,' or 'I turned my own driving wheels using a Dremel.' We need to know more. So rather than pitch you in at the deep end with some hands-on practical stuff, I thought we'd begin with a gallery of images; I'll be your guide, picking out points of interest as we stroll round.

***Right:** The liveries of industrial locomotives could be indecently garish, so the bright blue of this Neilson 0-4-0ST seems almost restrained.*

***Below:** In my experience, locomotive kits don't come any better than the High Level model of the Great Eastern Railway Class 209, later the LNER 'Y5'. For refinement of detail and staggering accuracy – not to mention the supremely confident fit of every component – this etched kit is in a league of its own. This one was built straight from the box by the eye-wateringly talented Tom Mallard and the GER livery was applied by the similarly gifted Chris Wesson – some pedigree! Looking at the photograph, I find it hard to believe that this model is in 4mm scale and barely three inches long overall. I wanted the impression of a grubby, dusty shunting locomotive kept busy among the wharves and warehouses of east London. Most of the weathering is concentrated on the smokebox, tank top and running gear, while the cab and saddletank look as though they receive at least an occasional going-over with an oily rag – here simulated by taking off the overspray with a flat brush, tissues and cotton buds, leaving a streaky residue here and there.*

Left: Industrial locomotives are there to work for a living, not to look pretty. This model of the NCB's Andrew Barclay 0-6-0T (1338/1913) revives some wonderful memories of the final years of steam operation in the Scottish coalfields, which I much preferred to the drabness of the blue diesel era on BR. The weathering treatment is absolutely straightforward and the soft lighting brings out the delicate burnishing of the Metalcote Gunmetal on the smokebox and boiler, giving the all-important metallic look. Another High Level kit, built in P4.

Above: There is a common misapprehension that pre-Grouping locomotives were always maintained in immaculate condition – they weren't, as the study of archive photographs will quickly confirm. Labour may have been cheap and plentiful but the railways still had a job to do and engine cleaning was not a major priority, except perhaps for express locomotives. Cleaning materials, moreover, were pretty primitive – just rags and cotton waste, with paraffin to get the dirt off and tallow to make the paintwork shine. Bob Hetherington models the Stockton & Darlington Railway in P4 and I've had the pleasure of weathering a number of his locomotives in workaday condition. The 2-4-0 passenger engine **Edward Pease** *(named after one of the original directors of the S&D) clearly works for a living, its bright Darlington livery contrasting with a general sootiness, the scuff marks on the tender and the paint chips on the steps from the crew's heavy boots.*

Below left: I have absolutely no idea of how many locomotives I've built over the years, but very few of them have been finished in such spotless condition as this BR Standard class 5 4-6-0, from the Alan Gibson kit. Like most of my black engines, the basis of the paint finish is Halford's acrylic satin black, sprayed directly from a rattlecan without a primer. The lining is from Fox Transfers. Look carefully though and you'll see clear signs of usage – the firebox, the cab roof, the tender. The boiler has been well cleaned but the polishing is far from even. In the late 1950s – no warning flashes, see? – No 73044 was a Patricroft engine regularly rostered on trans-Pennine expresses over both the Calder Valley and Standedge routes; contemporary photographs suggest it merited particular attention from the cleaners.

Right: Named after its birthplace, tiny Hudswell Clarke 0-4-0ST Leeds carries LMS crimson lake livery (Ford Lacquer Red from a Halford's spraycan over a white primer). Even with a Bob Moore pen, putting scale lining on such a diminutive engine is no easy task and I wasn't going to obscure most of it with a heavy weathering job. Instead, I wafted a gentle mist of my usual black/leather mix over the bits that mattered. Any overspray (which is inevitable) was wiped off the lined-out areas (or most of them) with a cotton bud. The 2ft 3in-diameter wheels, frames and smokebox all show signs of careful cleaning, but notice that the underside of the boiler remains characteristically untouched. I built this P4 model from a High Level kit, writing the instructions as I went.

Above: I finished my model of the LNER Hush Hush as it looked in its final months before withdrawal from active service. The weathering has the secondary effect of showing off the complex shape of the 'W1' and its impressive Art Deco styling. This experimental locomotive gave the operating department no end of trouble and by this time they weren't devoting any more time to its appearance than they had to, which is why ingrained dirt is starting to show all over the bodywork, especially around the front end and the cab. The locomotive body and frames are from the South Eastern Finecast kit; the tender body is from DJH, as the Finecast tender is nothing like any LNER eight-wheel tender, and there is a lot of scratchbuilding, modification and improvisation.

Right: Subtle gradations of grey and brown suggest this ex-Lancashire & Yorkshire 'pug' spent its working life well out of the limelight, tucked away in obscure goods yards and among dockside warehouses. I wanted to suggest years of indifference to its external appearance and my guide was an R. C. Riley portrait of the same engine, in London Midland Steam in Colour. Studied objectively, the steps look a little too airbrushed and might have benefitted from some random scrapes and abrasions – and yet this is exactly as they appear in my reference photograph. No 51218 was quite a wanderer and, prior to being bought for preservation, had been a Western Region engine for some years. Robin Whittle used a High Level chassis kit to convert this Dapol model for his P4 layout of Bristol Barrow Road.

Early diesels leaked oil everywhere. The sheen on this P4 model of the experimental ex-LMS Bo-Bo No 10800 was achieved by spraying a thin wash of Humbrol Metalcote Gunmetal over the base weathering on the bodyside panelling. Note that some areas remain matt – the radiator grille, cab roof and walkways, for instance. This is a Dave Alexander whitemetal kit on a scratchbuilt chassis. The open cab window – like the blue of the North British worksplate – is one of those little touches that do so much to bring a model to life.

I've always liked the styling of the dismally unsuccessful North British Type '1s', which were a direct linear development of the 10800. Stratford's fitters had a hard time with these pilot scheme locomotives and I don't think their outward appearance would have been of much concern – just keeping them going was challenge enough. This is another Dave Alexander whitemetal kit, this time on a BullAnt chassis. The weathering treatment is pretty standard, focussing once more on a dingy oiliness over sooty Brunswick green.

Left: Two-tone BR green seemed to further accentuate the oiliness of many early diesels. Here we have a grubby Heljan Class 47, Isambard Kingdom Brunel, earning its keep on a ballast train in an equally workaday factory setting. The buildings are adapted from HO-scale modular kits by DPM and Walthers; if anything, they look slightly cleaner than the locomotive. Thanks to rain and the Clean Air Act, industrial buildings – from factory units to engine sheds – were rarely quite as filthy as many modellers seem to portray them.

Below: From the evidence of contemporary photographs – black and white as well as colour – the prototype Deltic was not always maintained in immaculate condition, especially when it moved to the Eastern Region in 1959. There were usually some grubby patches on the bodysides, especially around the doors and footholds, and the roof always looked sooty. Even when it was new, the roof grilles were not a solid light grey as they are on the Bachmann model, so ome localised touching-in is called for.

Right: An airbrush is a fantastic tool for weathering, allowing you to build up all kinds of subtle effects. What it cannot replicate, however, are the random marks and abrasions that abound on the prototype. This is where more humble tools have their uses. The signs of rubbing on the cab door were added by smearing on a tiny dab of well-thinned grey with my little finger and scraping it with the nail. The scrapes and scuff marks – copied, as ever, from photographs – were put on with a clapped-out paintbrush that was down to its last four or five bristles. A quick stab and a twist and I had the effect I was after. The oil leakages were achieved by working wet paint with a damp brush flicked not downwards, as you might expect, but up. The Hymek is a Heljan model, converted to P4 with Alan Gibson wheels.

Above and right: The 'Western' class of diesel hydraulics were magnificent-looking locomotives but their handsome appearance depended on their being kept clean. Outward signs of neglect may have enhanced some classes – 'Peaks' and '25s' for instance, just as much as 'WDs' and '9Fs' – but a really filthy 'Western' just looked awful. My P4 model of Western Legionnaire (a Heljan model with Alan Gibson wheels and a Brassmasters dress-up kit) takes things about as far as they can go before they begin to look unpleasant. The vertical streaking on the sides is copied from photographs and serves to break up the uniformity and smoothness of moulded sides that do not ripple like the prototype.

Left: I love the vivid colours of India, evinced by the garish appearance of the Darjeeling Himalayan Railway's ancient B-class 0-4-0STs; their crudely applied blue paint is as vulgar as anything you would find at a fairground. The challenge with this 4mm-scale model (built from the Backwoods Miniatures kit) was to match the tarty paint with the hot, metallic and undeniably battered appearance of the working parts. I made extensive use of Metalcote Gunmetal on the smokebox and cylinders, but left the cab roof flat; the motionwork is liberally varnished to represent oil. To create the impression of a recent repaint, the blue was added last and given a quick wash of grime that was immediately wiped off the tank and cabsides (though the dome remained untouched), creating the effect of enthusiastic but not especially effective cleaning.

Top: *Consistency and continuity are important if you are going to spend several years building a model railway. Although it may be hard to tell from the photograph, these two 'Jinties' were built 20 years apart. The weathering is what links them together – both locomotives were painted using similar techniques and colours, by the same hands and, more importantly, the same pair of eyes. The one on the left dates from the mid-1980s and was my first attempt at a compensated chassis, using a Hornby body stripped down to the core and massively reworked with Riceworks fittings to represent one of the early locomotives without the distinctive 'keyhole'. The one on the right was completed in 2005 and has the then-new Bachmann bodyshell (again, much got-at with full cab interior and a Brassmasters detailing/upgrade kit) sitting on a High Level chassis.*

Middle top: *This 8F is a Hornby model that has been upgraded with Brassmasters detail parts. The weathering is pretty standard apart from the freshly repainted smokebox. This was common practice in London Midland workshops when the scale of repairs did not warrant a full repaint – smokeboxes could get very hot and the paint frequently blistered, causing further corrosion. As always, observation is the key to picking up on details such as this – but be aware that what was standard practice in one part of the country was not necessarily the same elsewhere. Scottish and North Eastern Region sheds, for instance, went in for improvised smokebox-door embellishments in a big way – blue-, red- or orange-backed numberplates and silver-painted door straps, for instance – but this became progressively less common the further south you went. On the strictly conformist Western Region, such individualistic touches were almost unknown.*

Middle bottom and bottom: *On balance, multiple-units tend to be cleaner than locomotives. This was as true when they were first introduced in the 1950s as it is on today's privatised railways, where they bring much-needed visual variety to a severely limited traction scene. Like coaching stock they are seen as corporate ambassadors for their operators, so they pass regularly through carriage-washing plants although their roofs and running gear are invariably left untouched. The green-liveried Metropolitan-Cammell unit is a DC Kits model, completed about a week before Lima announced their RTR version. The sides of the Lima class 156 are pretty clean and colourful but the rest is characteristically grubby. The model has been upgraded with Hurst Models' detailing parts.*

Right: Single unit four-wheel railcars were easy to keep clean – it's rare to find a shot of one looking grubby. My P4 reworking of the old Anbrico kit for the AC Cars unit has a sooty roof and a work-stained underframe, but on the whole it looks pretty presentable. I can easily imagine this unit on the Kemble-Tetbury branch being washed down once a week with a mop and bucket.

Below right: Roy Jackson built this EM gauge B16/1 – seen approaching the crossing at the south end of Retford station – from a Stephen Barnfield kit, with lining by Geoff Kent. We agreed on an ex-works finish, as if running in after overhaul at Darlington, with the weathering concentrated on the running gear, smokebox and cab roof – always the first parts of a locomotive to start to look dirty. I streaked the boiler and tender sides with Johnson's Klear floor polish, which breaks up the reflections and helps suggest the ripples and other surface irregularities that build up over the years on thin sheet metal – as befitting a locomotive built more than 35 years earlier. In some workshops it was the practice for motionwork, once it had been rubbed down to the bare metal, to be protected by a thick coat of grease, which I've represented here by a wash of tan-coloured gloss.

Left: The appearance of a new locomotive is not quite as we imagine it – especially if we take the way that an out-of-the-box model looks as our benchmark. The '47s' always bored me rigid, but I loved the sound of the 16-cylinder General Motors engines in the Class 57 rebuilds and immediately wanted a model of one. Freightliner Phoenix is a reworked Heljan Class 47 – the RTR model was still some years in the future when I built it – and is painted to represent a locomotive not long out of the Falcon works at Loughborough. The roof and running gear are already looking grubby and there is a characteristically oily sheen to the louvres. The bodyside streak was airbrushed on through a stencil and then worked with a barely damp brush; the smudgy finish to the translucent roof panels was copied from photographs.

Right: Great Rocks is one of only a very few engines I've weathered using the 'slosh and brush-up' technique, which involves slapping on a layer of thin, very wet paint all over the bodysides and then wiping most of it off again with cotton buds, tissues and paint brushes. It seems to take forever, though it does give you some excellent random marks. If you don't yet own an airbrush, this technique is a very good way of practising the subtle hand and eye coordination that is essential to successful weathering. The '37's' roof and underframe, however, were weathered conventionally using the airbrush. Lima's minimal tumblehome at the bottom of the bodysides was accentuated by airbrushing a heavy build-up of dirt in this area, exactly as per prototype. The eye reads this as an authentic turn-under, but it's basically just an optical illusion.

Above and left: *My P4 model of* Combe Martin *is one of my favourites. It's a semi-scratchbuild (the basic hulk of a Hornby bodyshell is under the hand-riveted 5-thou panelling, plus part of a Kitmaster tender body), though the complexities of its flywheel drive system need not concern us here. I wanted the model to reflect the real locomotive as it was when it moved to the Somerset & Dorset Railway in 1951, hence the rippled bodywork – so very different to a plastic moulding – and the overall cleanliness. Weathering is concentrated on the wheels, motionwork, ashpan area and, above all, the top of the casing – I have never yet seen a picture of a Bulleid Pacific in everyday service with a clean 'lid'. Randomly painting some areas of the bodywork with gloss acrylic varnish and others with satin helps break down the uniformity of the finish and accentuates the subtly different planes of the bodyside panels. When the 'Merchant Navy' class were new they were painted matt green, which didn't show up these irregularities but proved very difficult to keep clean. Eventually (and reluctantly), a conventional gloss finish was adopted.*

Below left: *Black '5s' were desperately boring engines – I saw hundreds of the things, so I should know – and unless you take care to individualise your models, they risk being equally dull. This is a Hornby model that's been treated to a Brassmasters dress-up kit. Note the way the lining is partly obscured, while the boiler bands have been knocked right back. The running plate, cab roof and top of the boiler are a slightly lighter colour to create false highlights, as if reflecting the sky. To my eye, the condition of this locomotive – neither particularly clean nor spectacularly filthy – is typical of BR steam until about 1965. After this date, things went a bit haywire and all pretence of maintenance seems to have been abandoned, other than odd locomotives that were cleaned by enthusiasts, sometimes on one side only (for photographic purposes). As often as not, they exhibited white buffers and other crude embellishments to the paintwork. Smokebox numberplates were optional by then, nameplates unlikely.*

Below: *As with the Black '5', I've given due attention to the bunker and tender top on this 'Crab', using a mixture of airbrushing and rust-coloured weathering powders. Coal is an acidic, highly abrasive mineral that makes short work of any surfaces it comes into contact with. It quickly eats through paint and attacks the bare metal beneath. There may be a bit of coal dust blowing around but bunkers are rust-red, not black.*

Right: *Having built a model of Falcon virtually by hand a few years back – scratch-built sprung chassis (with no fewer than six gearboxes), brutalised Q-kits fibreglass bodyshell and a mass of custom detail etchings – I feel Heljan's interpretation is a lot better than many modellers give credit for. The colours conflict with my memories of its lime green and chestnut livery, but otherwise all it needs is a bit of road dirt around the bogies and fuel tanks and some localised blackening of the grilles and louvres.*

Above: *With few crevices in which dirt could lodge, the slab sides of the Class '60s' should have been easy to keep clean but they seldom were. On my model of An Teallach – little but the basic bodyshell remains of the Lima original – coal fines have washed down from the roof and there is the characteristic oil seepage from the radiator compartment.*

Below: *Subtle changes of tone and hue – emphasised by black and white photography – are evident in this P4-converted BR Standard 2-6-4T. Weathering effects are rarely uniform on the prototype and neither should they be on models. On the other hand, marked contrasts should be avoided like the plague.*

Below and below right: *Most layouts are viewed from above rather than at eye-level, but top-down views showing the roofs of diesel locomotives are surprisingly hard to find and I struggled to find good reference material for these FIA Trains models of the LMS 'twins'. An added problem with the black and silver pair was locating images of any kind that reflected the desired degree of grubbiness. The green engines were easier in this respect, but I still relied largely on intuition and the general pattern in terms of detail weathering – oiliness around the exhaust outlets, seepage from the engine-compartment doors, lighter/darker patches appearing almost at random along the roofline. Because FIA Trains didn't do a 10000 in this particular late livery variant, I had to rework a model of 10001 and get rid of the warning panels. Some small details also needed modification – the two units were far from identical at any stage of their lives.*

Above: I love weathering WDs – the real thing displayed a degree of dirtiness that verged on the heroic and I enjoy replicating this on my models. I must have done a dozen or more by now – '9Fs' come a close second – but rather than adopting a generic style, 90297 is very much a 'portrait'. Details such as the limescaling on the boiler and the corroded smokebox should be faithfully copied from actual engines.

Left: Observant eyes are an important tool in weathering. One fairly common feature of steam days was the way in which lubricating oil from the cylinders would emulsify and spray out all over the leading wheels and the motionwork. This looks terrific when the locomotive is in action.

Left: Johnson's Klear floor polish applied over a light coat of weathering – localised darkening of the green sections is especially important – gives a well-polished look to this Hornby 'Britannia'.

Left: Generally speaking, the British sun isn't powerful enough for colour fading to be much of a problem, but its effects are noticeable on locomotives that go for many years without repainting – blue-liveried 08s and 37s especially. (Later on, I'll show you how I faded an EWS 08 using acrylic filters.) Bleaching is much more obvious in hot countries and I've replicated the effect on this Santa Fe SD40-2, so that it appears to have spent many years in the California sun. The red marks on the mid-carbody are where heat from the dynamic brakes has burned off the paintwork – a common feature on US locomotives handling huge trains on steep gradients.

A Prototypical Approach to Weathering

Why weather models? Well, why ever not?

My approach to model railways sees the layout as a totality. It represents a particular place during a particular period, with appropriate scenic details. Though the location may be fictitious, the railway itself will offer an accurate portrait of the type of trackwork, signalling, ballasting and infrastructure that would be found in such a place at such a time. The trains that run on that railway will be equally prototypical representations of those you would see on that line in the chosen timescale, and they will operate according to authentic protocols and plausible timetables.

Even if I am building a locomotive for a model railway that as yet does not exist, I'll still bear in mind the overall character and quality of the layout and will finish the model accordingly. Not everyone shares this view. There are different kinds of railway modellers, pursuing various levels of interest. There are the collectors who like to keep things in mint conditions, boxed and exactly as they are – not least in order to preserve the perceived value. There are the layout-builders who want to create a fantasy version of the world as they see it, which may not bear much relation to the world you or I see. (But so what? At least they're doing something constructive.) There are the cupboard modellers dreaming of building a layout, who acquire a lot of equipment but, for one reason or another, never manage to lay an inch of track or run a train – but assure us that, when they do, it will be to a standard that you and I can only dream of.

I don't imagine that many people in these categories will be reading this book. It is intended for those hands-on people who want to own and operate models whose appearance is so convincing that they might, if only for a fraction of a second, seem synonymous with the real thing – or at the very least offer a momentary connection with the real world, in all its glory and with all its flaws and blemishes. It is to such modellers that this book is addressed. Beyond the most basic train-set level, the urge to make our locomotives, stock, trackwork and scenic features as realistic as possible is the primary goal.

I hear some modellers complaining bitterly that the latest Hornby or Bachmann masterpiece has one rivet too few on the cab roof, or the wrong shape of guard irons. Yet they're perfectly happy to run it on their layout exactly as it comes out of the box, in its neat and ludicrously unprototypical semi-matt finish, unblemished by any sign of the routine wear and tear that affects all man-made objects.

Unweathered models, however beautifully made, are missing one key element of realism. They may have the right number of wheels with the right number of spokes; they may have perfectly-formed chimneys and domes; they may have see-through louvres and finely etched grilles, but the finish on them is completely

To many modellers, accustomed to a generic style of weathering, it still seems quite radical to think of copying prototype effects to create a portrait of an individual locomotive at a particular time. In the late 1980s, when Ian Metcalfe created this still talked-about Lima-based model of a class 50 on its last legs, such an approach was virtually unknown – at least in the UK. American modellers, however, were already looking at ways of achieving prototype-specific weathering – in some cases, according it the attention to detail normally associated with rivet-counting. Ian Metcalfe

Right: An 08 ticks over in the yard at Dewsbury Midland on the layout of the Manchester Model Railway Club. The whole scene has a beautifully relaxed, naturalistic quality enhanced by the banality of the setting. Everything is in harmony with everything else, including the nicely understated weathering.

unnatural. Some vital dimension is lacking. Though I may marvel at the level of craftsmanship, I feel as uncomfortable with this kind of shop-window model as I would watching a team taking the field for the Cup Final in last week's muddy kit.

Here's an illustration of my point. A 4mm layout that I'm familiar with has a wonderfully naturalistic and unforced finish. The track and lineside structures all look the part – with gently faded buildings, ragged grass on the embankments, brownish ballast. Occasionally, visitors are allowed to run their own engines and stock on this railway, and one day someone brought along a truly beautiful locomotive for a spin with a long rake of coaches, all professionally built and painted to the highest standard imaginable. The total cost must have been well into four figures. However, while the quality of the modelling hit you smack on the forehead, the train's immaculate finish was completely out of place on such a layout. For all its many virtues, it simply looked like a toy – albeit the kind of toy that looks very superior indeed and makes me envious of those who can afford such things.

The finish of a model locomotive is its outermost layer of skin, the first thing that we see. If there's something about that finish that displeases us – if it's too shiny, for instance, or it's patently the wrong colour – then we register this fact immediately. If the EWS maroon is too dark (as it often is) or too flat (ditto), it can be very difficult to see beyond the finish and take in the other qualities of the model, even if the detail is excellent and the general outline is accurate.

But give a model a believable and acceptable finish and we see at once through the thin outer layer of paint, to consider other aspects of the model – such as how well, or otherwise, it captures the features and character of the prototype. This is where good weathering scores, because even a not-so-good model (a Lima Class 37 or 47, for instance) will suddenly start to look much more

Below: Another fine example of integrated modelling – one of Colwick's characteristically filthy WD 2-8-0s shunts the coal yard at Southwell Central on John Sutton's acclaimed 3mm layout. The overall portrait of down-at-heel railway facilities serving a small Nottinghamshire town is achieved as much by the subtle qualities of the painting as by the actual modelling. Everything is given the same level of attention – from the limestreaking on the locomotive to the empty sacks thrown casually over the coal bins on the right – but nothing is allowed to draw attention to itself. This is a layout I have operated on many occasions and the running is as flawless as its appearance. Apart from a few wagons made from kits, everything you see in this image is built from scratch.
John Sutton

Peter Johnson is another modeller with an intuitive feeling for his subject – in this case, a run-down slice of dockside life (Gloucester? Goole? Ellesmere Port?) on his hugely atmospheric EM-gauge layout, Canada Road. In my view, Peter suggests the essential squalor of the blue-diesel era better than anyone else. Once again everything in the picture – including the wagons – is scratch built apart from the Hornby locomotive, which has had an awful lot done to it. In half a century of railway modelling, the semi-sunken barge is one of the best things I've ever seen.
Philip Sutton

plausible. We see a nice weathering job and we think, 'Yes, that rings a bell' – in which case, we may not immediately (if at all) notice the steamroller wheels or the absence of front-end pipework.

Good weathering will never fully hide the faults of a bad model, but it will certainly mitigate them. With a decent base model as your starting point, it will push it to new heights of realism. This is why weathering is necessary, or indeed essential; to ignore its possibilities it to deny yourself the option of bringing a whole new range of improvements and enhancements to your models.

However, weathering should never draw attention to itself. It should be nonchalant, appropriate, as expected. We shouldn't especially notice it because it should be so much of a piece with everything around it. It may please the eye, but it should never stand out. Good weathering, like a good waiter, is amazingly unobtrusive – which is not to say it should be invisible. It should merely be suitable to its context, whether it's a filthy WD on a coal train at the very end of steam or a slightly sooty auto-train on a Great Western branch line.

One final point – does weathering lower the sell-on value of a model? I'm not sure. Bad weathering is no enhancement, certainly, but a couple of years back on American eBay a bidding frenzy broke out to secure a beautifully weathered ATSF C40-8W. It was otherwise a not especially brilliant, out-of-the-box Bachmann model worth $40, tops, but, with its tattered paintwork fading almost to pink, this HO-scale beauty finally went for the thick end of $600. That's nothing – you'll need 20 times that amount to buy a hand-built O gauge model by Tony Reynalds or Lee Marsh – the Stanley Beesons of the 21st century, the absolute top of their particular tree – and it will come to you ready-weathered as a matter of course. Their builders wouldn't have it any other way, and neither would their customers.

A question of degree

What do we mean by weathering? To the uninitiated, it means making a model look as though someone's dunked it in mulligatawny soup and then dropped a bag of soot on it. It means dabbing rust patches on to squeaky-clean paintwork and having white streaks of limsescale pouring down from every conceivable aperture. It suggests locomotives and rolling stock that appear to have passed through a quagmire on their short journey from the fiddle yard to the branch terminus. To the collector, it means ruining a perfectly good model and making serious inroads into its value.

Below: Weathering in action – rain trickles down the casing of a Bulleid Light Pacific, bringing with it an accumulation of soot, ash, oil and road dirt. This is what causes the characteristic streaking.

Bottom: The same thing happening on a preserved 'Peak'.

Above: An authentic-looking freight locomotive – 90705 exhibits the WD's characteristic all-over coating of grime as it works light through Rutherglen in the early 1960s. There is very little variation of tone but the effect is far from uniform. Author's collection

Weathering, as I practise it, means none of these things. It is primarily concerned with enhancing the appearance of models, making them look more believable through the careful build-up of effects that signify wear and tear, wind and rain, smoke and dust. If you don't notice it, if it looks so natural that the models blend in with the layout as a whole, that's because you're on the way to recognising railway modelling as an art form.

Top: Different forms of traction weather in similar ways, as shown by this end-of-steam scene at Gloucester (Horton Road).

So what kind of weathering are we after? There's a myth that, before about 1960, locomotives on the whole were kept in very good external condition. The further back through the century you go, supposedly, the cleaner those engines were – until, by about 1900, they must have positively hurt your eyes because they gleamed so brightly.

Why do people have this impression of an army of engine cleaners who spent their working lives polishing locomotives – shunting pugs and freight locomotives as well as top-link power? There's no archive record that such a thing ever happened. Until the last few years of film photography, materials were expensive and most railway photographers – especially in the inter-war period and earlier – preferred to save their film for prestige expresses and the more attractive locomotives and workings. But if you look at the work of, say, H. C. Casserley and W. A. Camwell – two pioneering recorders of the steam railway who travelled the length and breadth of the country, photographing everyday scenes at stations and engine sheds – you'll see that, in their commonplace pre-war world, locomotives (and railways generally) were nothing like as clean as we imagine them to be. In fact, on the whole they were just as grubby and neglected as they were when I first became aware of railways in the late 1950s.

Above: The very end of steam – corroded and unkempt, but still with well-oiled motionwork. 92022 has just been shunted onto the scrap line at Birkenhead on 4 November 1967 and is only just about in steam. Note the late tender change from the high-sided BR1B to the inset BR1G.

However, main-line express locomotives were kept a lot cleaner than they would be soon after. Though there were always exceptions (a gleaming 'Brit' was a rare sight), the Pacifics I saw regularly at places like Crewe, York and Doncaster tended to look pretty good. I remember brightly-polished 'Kings' at Wolverhampton Low Level and immaculate streaks on the prestigious East Coast mainline expresses. I still expected main-line power to look the part, but even while I was still modelling in three-rail I can also recall dingy 'Duchesses' on the 'Royal Scot' and 'Caledonian', filthy 'A3s' at King's Cross, shabby-looking Bulleids at Nine Elms – and I have the photographs to confirm my impressions. Lesser top-link and secondary passenger power – 'Scots' and 'Jubilees', for instance, or 'B1s' and 'V2s' – tended to be clean but not scrupulously so. By modelling standards they'd be considered quite well weathered.

*Rust patches
were common on
vulnerable areas such
as smokeboxes,
bunkers and tender
sides, less so on
other parts of a
steam locomotive.*

*Diesels rust too,
though finding such
marked corrosion on
a unit as modern as
this GBRf Class 66 is
unusual.*

When diesels and electrics arrived, they were only immaculate when new. The kind of thorough cleaning and titillating associated with Top Shed 'A4s' or Old Oak's 'Castles' was unknown, even with their direct replacements – the 'Deltics' and 'Westerns' (although the Finsbury Park 'Deltics' were polished by hand for a while). Engines might have been given a perfunctory sluicing-down in a washing plant, but it rarely went any further. Roofs and bogies were always mucky. Freight stock has never, to my knowledge, been cleaned by any railway under the sun; coaches are cleaned no more than is strictly necessary, and then only the colourful bits.

It was much the same when green gave way to blue and, in turn, to all kinds of pre- and post-privatisation liveries. Triple-grey Railfeight is a perfect livery for showing off dirt and faded paintwork. GBRf seem to make an effort but do EWS/ DB Schenker actually clean their engines at all? The modern traction magazines, however, seem to perpetrate the myth of clean, colourful locomotives operating in a Britain of perpetual summer. ('Because that's what people like to see,' the former editor of one such magazine tells me.) This isn't how it is, as an hour or so at Arpley, Ipswich or Peak Forest will soon tell you.

Look back a century or so and there are many, many pictures of gleaming Midland compounds and Great Western outside-framed 4-4-0s with poetic names. The pictorial albums are full of such images, most of which have a posed quality; on the rare occasions when you find more spontaneous photographs, the engines are not always particularly clean, which to me suggests a truer picture of how things were.

*Paint fades into
interesting and
unusual colours.
I hesitate to put a
name to this well-
weathered shade –
khaki beige, perhaps,
or donkey brown
with a hint of sage
green?*

It's the same with the newly liveried locomotives you see every month in *Rail Express* or *Traction* – they got photographed because they made for a nice picture, not because they were in any way representative of things overall. Just look at the photographs in an Ian Allan ABC, or in Casserley and Asher's monumental *Locomotives of British Railways*. Enthusiasts taking record photographs of obscure locomotive classes didn't put their cameras away because the rarities they travelled hundreds of miles to see were just as grubby as the common-or-garden classes nearer home.

The best modelling captures a sense of the everyday – as did the great *Picture Post* photographers such as Bill Brandt and Bert Hardy. But most people don't record the humdrum aspects of their lives – they only get their cameras out for weddings, Christmas parties and family holidays, when everyone looks their best. No one takes photographs of their friends and relatives getting out of bed in the morning, trying to find their glasses or shopping at the supermarket. No one (to the best of my knowledge) has ever photographed me asleep or at

Green-liveried 'Deltics' could be just as filthy as any steam locomotive. D9017, still unnamed in August 1963, stands at York with an express for King's Cross.

Below: The yellow ends have been cleaned to make the locomotive more visible, but this Class 37 looks tired and shabby as it sits out Sunday at Colchester TMD in the mid-1980s. Few liveries were as unflattering as corporate blue, especially once the inevitable fading had set in. I found the blue-diesel era oddly dispiriting – it bespoke an increasingly scruffy railway that seemed unable or unwilling to move forward. The transition period of the1960s had been dynamic and exciting, as the pre- and post-privatisation eras would be, but there was not much to enthuse about in between times.

work or reading a book or building a model, but these four activities alone have accounted for a high proportion of my time on Earth.

I think it's much the same with early railway photographs. Many of the vintage pictures reproduced in books and magazines are 'officials', designed to give the right impression. There are plenty of shots of newly-completed express locomotives, but rather fewer showing humble goods engines in late middle age – and of those that do exist, the locomotives look less than spruce. Photographs of engine cleaners hard at work were a great favourite of Big Four publicists, but in a decade of steam-era train-spotting, encompassing literally hundreds of depot visits, I only once remember seeing an engine being cleaned – a 'Crab' at Birkenhead. I was so surprised I took a photograph to record the event.

Remember also that those heroic engine cleaners of the pre-war period didn't have a kitchen cupboard of detergents to help them with their work. On the whole they got by with a bucket of water and some old rags – perhaps a mop, or some paraffin, if they were lucky. Polishing was done with an oily rag or tallow, not some lanolin-based care product that's as kind to your hands as it is to your furniture. So right from the start they were fighting a losing battle against filth, grime, coal dust, soot, ash, oil, dirty water, rust and all kinds of aggressive forces. It's hard enough to keep a car clean in our environmentally conscious age, so what chance was there for the steam locomotive operating in a far more polluted working environment?

Right: Heading up a weekend ballast at Colchester engineers' sidings, large-logo 37108 looks dusty but presentable while its Railfreight General partner has been partly cleaned at either end.

At the risk of oversimplifying matters and ignoring obvious overlaps, I think we
can break down the external condition of a locomotive into eight categories.

- **Brand new and freshly released from shops, or
  newly overhauled and fully repainted.**

- **Well cleaned for service on prestigious trains.**

*'Battle of Britain' 4-6-2 No 34089 602 Squadron is seen here looking
astonishing at Eastleigh, immediately after its November 1960 rebuilding (by
which time even the Southern had started applying electrification warning
flashes). To all intents and purposes, it's a new locomotive fresh out of the
box – but note the scuffed buffers and the protective oil coating on the
motionwork. It stands out like a sore thumb in its humdrum surroundings.*

*Two 'Castle' class 4-6-0s catch the early-morning light at Shrewsbury shed
c1961. No 4096 on the left has been well wiped over with an oily rag; by
contrast No 4085 is in more workaday condition, but the copper-capped
chimney still gleams and the green paintwork, while flat, is presentable.*

- **Prepared for special duties, showing exceptional
  levels of cleanliness.**

- **As above, but paintwork is clearly discoloured and
  lining/lettering beginning to fade.**

*'Schools' class 4-4-0 No 30915 Brighton was bulled up by Stewarts Lane
depot. Decidedly non-standard, especially for the drab 1950s, the clean-up
included a white cab roof and edging on the wheels and smoke deflectors.
The front coupling, handrails, motionwork and smokebox door hinges
have been taken back to bare metal. Brighton was always a pet engine
at Stewarts Lane and for many years the automatic choice for boat trains
and excursions – very possibly including, in this instance, the Royal Special
taking the newly crowned Queen Elizabeth II from Victoria to Tattenham
Corner for the Derby on 6 June 1953. R N H Hardy*

*A delightful portrait of one of the neat '1366' class 0-6-0PT engines at
Wadebridge c1962, shortly after they ousted the Beattie well tanks on the
china-clay line to Wenford Bridge. With its oily wheels and grubby buffer
beam it's clearly a working locomotive, though its cab and tanks (if not
its smokebox sides, running plate, sandbox operating rods and injector
pipework) have been well cleaned by conscientious footplatemen.*

- **Starting to show obvious signs of neglect, with dull paintwork.**

'Royal Scot' class 4-6-0 No 46129 The Scottish Horse, *looking decidedly grubby at Bletchley in 1962. Much of the lining is obscured and there's no hint of sparkle, except for the oil on the driving wheels. Oil residues – hurled out by centrifugal force and dried to a flat finish – coat the lower part of the locomotive. There is clear evidence of priming in the white deposits running down the firebox and smokebox. Lest it be assumed that this is a 'Beeching era' state of affairs, there are plenty of photographs of 'Big Four' express locomotives in this state.*

- **External appearance of no concern – lining and livery may be virtually obscured.**

Make your freight locomotives look like this and you won't go far wrong. 'Q6' 0-8-0 No 63360 – seen in the final months of steam at Tyne Dock in 1966 – looks as these great North Eastern workhorses did for most of their lives. Mechanically, they were always kept in perfect condition despite the neglect of their external appearance. This is another study rich in detail – the leaking tender tank, the rust on the coal rails, the ash shovelled out through the cab entrance, the dribble down the firebox and oil all over the wheels.

- **Not cleaned for some time, but otherwise apparently well-maintained.**

'H' class 0-4-4T No 31544, on shed at Tunbridge Wells West, is a study in fine weathering detail – from the oil-caked Westinghouse pump and the chalky deposits on the safety valves to the warm smokebox colours and the smudgy tank and bunker sides. Accentuated by the brilliant sunlight, these touches bring the locomotive to life as surely as the wisps of escaping steam.

- **Severely neglected and due for early withdrawal.**

With rusting smokebox and its upper works covered in soot and ash, only the steam drifting from the snifting valve suggests that K1 2-6-0 No 62011 has not yet reached the end of the road at North Blyth on 15 September 1966. In fact, this one-time stalwart of the West Highland line had another year to go before its final withdrawal and it is doubtful whether its external condition improved. The newly repainted smokebox door (a common feature of North Eastern Region engines that had suffered corrosion damage) shows just how dirty the rest of the engine had become.

Why (and How) Locomotives Weather

Real railway locomotives get dirty for a variety of reasons. It's quite a complicated three-dimensional equation, involving different things happening over time. So let's first of all consider a steam locomotive.

Almost as soon as it leaves the paint shop, the glossy paintwork will begin to turn dull, just as it will on a wagon, a carriage or any other item of railway equipment. This happens quite quickly, over a few weeks at most. The brightness of the livery colours will tone down and fade – this is a much more gentle process, but it will become noticeable after a couple of years, especially when compared with an ex-works example. Some colours – noticeably dark green, navy blue and some of the deeper reds – begin to assume a blackish tinge over time.

Regular cleaning will help preserve the paintwork on a locomotive, but wind and rain, sunlight, exposure to pollutants and chemical decomposition within the paint itself will inevitably take their toll on the once-pristine finish. Daily wear and tear and exposure to surface damage are also inevitable. The locomotive's appearance may still be presentable, but close inspection inevitably reveals dirt and discoloration in hard-to-access places, as well as local damage caused by scuffs and abrasions – kick marks on steps or a cab door, for instance.

If you got your impression of rail operations from the monthly magazines, this is how your models would look. Publicity-conscious repaints aside, none of today's private operators takes anything like the same care of their fleet's appearance that Mendip Rail and their predecessors did. However, both 59002 Alan J Day and 59004 Yeoman Challenger were freshly re-liveried when photographed at Berkeley on 29 May 1996 and 12 August 2003 respectively.

You can see this happening on a preserved locomotive that has been stuffed and mounted outdoors. Even if the engine hasn't moved an inch in years, the paintwork will look flat and it will also carry clear vertical streaks where rain has washed down the boiler, the cab and the water tank(s) or tender. There will be splash marks at ground level where water has hit the ground and bounced back. In fact, any painted metal object exposed to the elements – be it a piece of machinery, a road vehicle or an item of garden furniture – will betray similar characteristics over time.

In addition to the effects of time, weather and atmosphere on the paintwork, a working steam locomotive will soon start to show clear evidence of its daily occupation. Smoke and steam will beat down on the top of the boiler and the cab roof, discolouring the paintwork. Ash and cinders will be thrown out of the chimney and some will fall on the boiler, the running plate and other areas. (The footplate, by the way, will be swept rather than cleaned because a shiny, slippery running plate is a hazard for enginemen.)

When the locomotive passes through tunnels, age-old soot encrustations may be dislodged by the exhaust – this still happens today, half a century after steam power ceased on many lines, hence the sooty roofs ubiquitously found on diesel and electric traction. As the locomotive continues on its journey, rain will further act on these deposits, washing them down the side of the engine in dirty streaks. The longer the locomotive goes without being properly cleaned – and you often see evidence of the top section of a boiler not being wiped over – the more pronounced these effects will be.

Dirt from the track will also be thrown up by the wheels as the train moves along. You can see this very graphically as reddish vertical streaks on the ends of wagons, but on a locomotive this road dirt is more likely to collect as an all-over coating on the spokes and wheel rims, frames and cylinders, cab and tender steps and other areas below footplate level. Here it will mingle with a fine coating of red-oxide particles from the brake blocks until the whole of the underframe area appears to be an ochre colour, showing only the subtlest variations of tone. Again, these effects start to show very quickly and intensify over time.

Steam locomotives use a lot of oil and some of this inevitably finds its way onto the exposed outer surfaces, attracting dirt and encouraging the further build-up of deposits of road dust and brake-shoe particles – but never randomly, only in proximity to parts that have been over-oiled and/or thrown their lubricant over the surrounding area. Over time, the effects of oil and corrosion will turn the valve gear and motionwork a rich brown colour, almost always glistening. Oil will build up on the wheels (usually fairly evenly on account of centrifugal action) and as thick deposits on the brake gear and tender axleboxes. Usually the latter will be a blackish colour, displaying various degrees of oiliness – sometimes it is shiny like gloss varnish, at other times it is dead matt.

Steam locomotives also consume many tons of coal and thousands of gallons of water. Coal is an acidic, highly corrosive mineral broken down into lumps with sharp edges. Consequently, tender coal spaces and bunkers take a hammering and are invariably rusty and battered – never black. Water is gentler in its action but no less liable to cause discoloration and deterioration. Rust will start to form around leaking joints, or where pipework and other fittings penetrate exterior surfaces; soon it will be washed downwards by gravity and form pronounced streaks. Fresh rust is a bright orange colour, but old rust is much darker and almost purplish in shade. Once again, these are effects that build up over time and they may not be present on all locomotives.

The lime deposits carried as a solution in very hard water will also cause streaking, often as dribbles from boiler fittings such as safety valves, washout plugs or clack valves. Impure water may cause the locomotive to prime and throw out large quantities of dirty water and limescale from the chimney, which will land on the boiler and cause a highly characteristic white streaking – sometimes on the smokebox alone, sometimes affecting the whole locomotive. This effect will not, however, generally be found on locomotives operating in areas where the water supply is naturally soft and low in lime content – in Yorkshire, for instance, and throughout most of Scotland.

And so it goes on. Enginemen's overalls will rub against grubby cabsides and doors (if fitted) and gently polish them; shiny brass whistles and safety valves (not forgetting nameplates) will quickly blacken; copper-capped chimneys likewise; heat will turn smokeboxes a dark silvery grey and may even burn the paint off altogether in the worst-affected areas (especially smokebox doors), exposing livid patches of corrosion; vermilion buffer beams will fade to pink. Obviously not all locomotives show the same characteristics at the same time, or weather at the same rate, but these broad patterns are immediately apparent from the close study of photographs or (better still) the real thing

Cleaning sometimes adds to rather than counteracts the effects of weathering. Often the pretty parts of a locomotives – those painted a specific 'livery' colour and/or lined out in a contrasting shade – will be given a wiping down, giving the impression of an engine that is well cared for. But the working parts of the locomotive – the wheels and motion, top of the boiler, cab roof and tender frames – will not be touched by the cleaner's rag. Even on an express engine, all these elements will generally be as unkempt as the grubbiest freight locomotive. It is rare indeed to see an engine that is clean from top to bottom.

Diesel locomotives – and to a lesser degree electrics – weather in surprisingly similar ways to their steam counterparts. There is a very interesting article by Brian Haresnape on this subject – suggesting the use of special livery colours to mitigate its effect – in the October 1966 issue of *Modern Railways*. The most noticeable discoloration is once again the organic dust around the wheels and running gear that builds up during the course of a journey, largely composed of tiny oxide particles from the brake shoes. It spreads itself as an even, brownish layer from rail level to waist – or sometimes higher – and can assume such proportions as to completely obliterate the livery colour. If this dust becomes mixed with oil – as on bogies, for example – it becomes more adhesive and noticeably darker in colour. Increased local discoloration will also be found around exhaust outlets and, to a lesser degree, on radiator grilles and louvres.

Without prompt attention, this slow accumulation of uncleaned residues will soon be evident all over the locomotive, particularly on the uneven surfaces of the bogies and undergear. Oil, seeping from the engine compartment or spilling down the bodyside, has a particularly disruptive visual effect. It quickly attracts blackening dirt and its streaks across the livery scheme – breaking up

37689, looking all of its 40-odd years, at Arpley TMD on 4 January 2005. The bodysides are scarred and pitted, the paint is flaking and the finish is totally flat.

Triple-grey Railfreight livery is just the ticket for showing how weathering effects build up. Note the subtle vertical streaking and the build-up of road dirt and brake-block dust on the lower bodysides.

In the late 1990s, Freightliner-owned 47292 was probably the shabbiest locomotive on the network. Its triple-grey livery was badly faded and there were ugly marks where its Railfreight brandings had been torn off. Despite appearances, it was apparently a reliable machine and popular with crews.

the carefully wrought system of lines, bands and colours – draw attention to unrelated portions of the locomotive, making them seem unduly prominent and grotesquely blemished. The effect is akin to camouflage – just look at an EWS Class 66 that has been used on railhead treatment duties.

The eye is automatically drawn to dirt and discoloration where it obscures fine detail, or alters its apparent shape. This is especially evident where lettering, numbers and symbols are affected, or where colour changes seem to become patchy and uneven. It is also one reason why triple-grey Railfreight livery with squadron markings – so stunning when newly applied – quickly degraded into shabbiness and squalor, accentuated by the rapid fade of the grey bodyside colours.

Mechanical washing plants utilising chemical solutions have been in use in Britain for many years, but they fail to provide a comprehensive solution to the problems of dirt build-up. They are fine with coaches and multiple-units but more problematical with locomotives. Projections and recessed areas on the bodywork collect dirt that evades mechanical washing techniques. Changes of plane – such as the transitional curve from bodyside to roof – will often present a graduated change from cleaned areas to a layer of dirt. This is a common sight on units with a high cantrail, and also on diesel classes such as the '37s', 'Westerns' and 'Warships'.

De-branded triple-grey Railfreight 56078 approaches Hatfield and Stainforth with a Bredbury-Roxby loaded binliner on 17 July 2002. Note the marks of rainwater on the cab roof, the brake-block dust on the flanks and the build-up of dirt in the recesses of an otherwise clean nose.

Electric locomotives and units suffer from a broadly similar discoloration, although there is far less oil spillage to darken the dirt layer. Ochre-coloured dirt build-up on the bogies and underframes is a common characteristic. With overhead supply systems, however, a greenish-grey deposit from the copper wire collects around the pantograph mountings and streaks the roof and ends, sometimes extending down the sides of the locomotive or unit.

This Class 90 was hastily repainted for the launch of the short-lived One livery, but no one bothered with the bogies and running gear which were as grubby as ever.

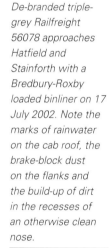

A Study in Weathering

You need to be at least 50 years old to have even the vaguest appreciation of what a working BR steam locomotive actually looked like. I'm glad so many of them survive, but I find they don't often capture the particular qualities of 'the real thing' – they look like the preserved locomotives they are and there's an air of artificiality about their appearance.

Even when they're in steam, they shine in the wrong places; they have burnished pipework; the paint looks too fresh and too intense; there are odd errors and inconsistencies in the lining and lettering, and customisations that would never have been contemplated in British Railways days. But it could be worse – to my eye, preserved coaches of the BR period always look wrong, whatever their livery.

So it was with considerable surprise and pleasure that I called in one autumn afternoon at Sheringham station on the North Norfolk Railway and found the sole surviving 'B12' 4-6-0 ready to pull out on a Holt train, looking very much the part. I took a sequence of photographs to remind myself of all the subtle details and nuances of colour that appear on different parts of a steam locomotive in service.

As can be seen in this three-quarter view, the livery of 61572 was actually far from being black. There's as much browny-grey in various shades as there is anything else, but notice how well everything harmonises. The cleanest parts – in fact the only clean parts – are the boiler, the splasher sides, the cab side sheets and the tender. Everything else is pretty mucky and yet the superficial impression is of a reasonably clean engine. Most of the cleaners' attentions have, as usual, been focused on the liveried areas such as the tender sides, cab and boiler. As has long been the custom, the running plate has merely been swept rather than cleaned, so as to provide a non-slip surface. Below the valances, the running gear has been left to the mercies of the elements and shows the gradual build-up of ash, oil, brake dust and other signs of use.

Above: Some gentle streaking is clearly visible on the boiler and smokebox, all the more apparent in close-up. Although nominally black, the two clearly exhibit different shades – the smokebox is obviously a hot area and has a much warmer tinge than the heavily lagged boiler. There is also spillage from the smokebox lubricator that has not been cleaned up.

Right: In all my years of watching trains, I don't think I've seen more than a handful of locomotives with shiny steel motionwork. The B12's coupling rods are a perfect weathering guide for modellers seeking a typical effect; note the oiliness, the vertical streaking and the subtle variegation of colour. Much of this is caused by how the light catches the rods but it's still worth capturing in paint. The running plate is dusty and the brake gear is covered in fine particles from the brake blocks, which are an orange-red colour very similar to (but not the same as) the general running-gear dirt.

Above: More near-monochrome track colour on the bogie, but also with gentle variations. Random oil spillages and spray accounts for the spotting on the leading wheel.

Left: The cab roof is, as always, a sooty brownish-black and there is a lot of reddish dust (brake-block particles) below the running plate. There is a small touch of rust on the cab roof, probably where the paint has been scuffed by a stray fire iron, and a similar mark at the back of the cab step where it's been repeatedly clouted by steel-capped boots. The lined black areas are clean, in a smudgy kind of way, but dirt has built up in the corners and other hard-to-access areas. The finish is neither matt nor glossy, but there is a still a sparkle to the paintwork and a highlight where the sun glints on the boiler. The working parts of the engine – the cab entrance and running gear – are clearly those of a locomotive that earns its keep, rather than a museum piece. There is very little colour variation in the weathering tones and what does exist is very subtle.

A Study in Weathering (continued)

Above: *The cleaner's rag has concentrated on the boiler cladding and missed out working parts such as the washout plugs, safety valves and whistle. The latter have a very metallic feel to them – not at all the gleaming brightwork of a model, more the deep, rich patina of a well-used piece of machinery. There is a touch of rust too, on account of water leaks and dribbles from the locomotive's plumbing arrangements.*

Above: *Weathering is subtle, as we know, but there is also a randomness to it that is very difficult to capture accurately. An airbrush is fine for adding a light dusting, but the arbitrary dings, scrapes and smudges seen in this view need to be added by hand. Study particularly the cab steps and the injector; the wheels and tender axlebox are quite oily but everything else is dead flat.*

61572 was clearly cleaned regularly. Shed staff were aware that, if you gave a bit of attention to certain key areas – generally those that were lined out or painted in a specific livery colour – then the engine as a whole would look well cared for. You can see this many times in photographs of express passenger and mixed-traffic engines from the time of the Big Four onwards. Freight engines, however, have always been another matter entirely . . .

Above: *The tender bodywork is pretty clean – all the lining is visible – but down below it's a different story. There is oil on the axleboxes, scuff marks on the steps and brake dust everywhere. Note the reddish brown of the brake shoes and yet how well it blends in with the rest of the tender underpinnings. The variations of tone are subtle and nothing particularly stands out.*

Middle: *Most people would regard this 'B12' as a well cared-for engine, but closer inspection reveals a familiar combination of cleanliness and grubbiness typical of steam locomotives since way back in the Victorian era. It looks nothing like an out-of-the-box model.*

Left: *Brake dust and track dirt coat the tender underframe in a monochromatic brown, but note that the encrustation is more pronounced in some areas. There is oil around the tender axleboxes and also, to a lesser degree, on the spring shackles and wheels. The latter show oily dribbles acquired while the engine was stationary for long periods.*

Equipment

I've often remarked at my weekend workshops that weathering is roughly 80% observation, 10% technique and 10% the tools you use. This may come as a disappointment to those for whom throwing money at state-of-the-art workshop equipment is as important as putting it to practical use, but this is the way it so often is with a creative hobby. Owning a Stradivarius soldering iron, as Allan Sibley once said, will not in itself make you a great model-maker.

Railway modelling is not by definition an expensive pastime and weathering is one of the areas where purchasing power counts for very little. Your eyes cost you nothing; learning a good technique takes time; only acquiring equipment involves money. Even then, the amount of expenditure is not great. You can learn the rudiments of weathering with little more than a couple of paintbrushes, some cans of paint and a few sachets of powder. For many years this was how I used to do things, before I had

a succession of budget-priced airbrushes. But even if you bought the best equipment on the market, you'd be looking at spending no more than a few hundred pounds – if that. Most people get by perfectly well without spending anything like this amount of money. The only thing really worthy of expenditure is a decent airbrush and such a piece of kit has, of course, many other applications in modelling.

Various techniques came together in weathering these two Bachmann locomotives – the treatment was similar but the individual application was quite different. This composite approach calls for a variety of tools, which we'll explore in this chapter. The way I do it, the airbrush is the main item of equipment involved, but there are also clapped-out paintbrushes, cotton buds, makeup applicators and even fingers.

Airbrushes

The main tool I use is a double-action airbrush. It's called this because the trigger works two ways – press it down to control the air supply, pull back to regulate the flow of paint. This gives you a degree of subtlety and makes things pretty simple in operation. In a single-action airbrush these functions are separated and the brush is not so easy to use; nor does it offer the degree of control to enable you to create delicate effects. I had a single-action airbrush for a year or two and, while I got some impressive results with it, the move up to a double-action design brought immediate and obvious benefits.

Which to choose? Beyond a certain basic level, there's probably not a vast difference between the various makes of airbrush. Paasche, DeVilbiss and Badger are the best-known brands. If you can run to one of these you won't go far wrong. Most people get used to whatever they have – they know what it can do, they're aware of its limitations and are not really conscious of the other options that may be available. But if you can afford something better, I don't see any merit in buying a cheap airbrush. There are some good budget-priced designs coming in at around £80 that can produce excellent results (the AB180 from *everythingairbrush.com* comes to mind), but many of the others are roughly made, pretty crude in operation and don't do a particularly good job. They will hold you back.

I have two airbrushes. One is a Badger 150, the default setting for many modellers (the guys I know are more likely to have a 150 than anything else). It's fine – it's reliable, it's comfortable to use, but it's a Ford Mondeo rather than a Mercedes. It has quite a wide spray pattern, so you can perform basic livery applications and scenic work with it, but you can also come in close and create some subtle weathering effects. Most modellers never gravitate beyond such an airbrush and, to be fair, they don't really need to. The 150 does require careful cleaning though. Mine came with fine and heavy-duty head/needle assemblies as well as the normal one; I thought this would be a wonderful advantage but in practice I only ever use the standard fittings.

My other airbrush is an Iwata HP-SB Plus. In automotive terms this is an Audi or Lexus; it's in a totally different class to the Badger because of the quality of its design and manufacture. It can perform the workhorse role for hour after hour, but its delicacy of control gives you many advantages in weathering applications. I bought one after exclusively using Badgers for many years and it was a revelation – it's extremely reliable (provided you clean and service it thoroughly) and wonderfully sensitive to the touch.

Another airbrush I've tried is the Aztek double-action design. It may look more like a Stanley knife than an airbrush but there's no doubting its abilities. Unlike most other makes, the needle and spring are housed within the nozzle itself rather than encased in the main body and can easily be accessed for cleaning. To change to a finer or coarser nozzle from the various spray pattern types available, simply unscrew one and install another. Access to the airbrush's innards is unnecessary (and also impossible). Professional weatherer Martyn Welch used an Aztek 470 day in, day out for years, which in normal hobbyist terms would amount to a century or more of service.

Buying an expensive airbrush will not, however, confer on you the kind of skills that Martyn has. These must be learned through practice, making mistakes and going down blind alleys. Someone who has at least some grasp of what they're trying to achieve, has a reasonable eye and knows which way round to hold an airbrush – even if it's not a top-of-the-range model – will always produce a better result than an ignoramus with an Iwata. That's a simple fact of life.

Above: This is the main airbrush I use, the Iwata HB-SP Plus. It's a double-action airbrush (press the trigger down for air, pull back for paint) with a small side-feed cup that can be fitted left or right – the blanking plug is visible here. Compared with anything else I've used, it has superb control of paint delivery and is beautifully balanced in my hand. You can paint a 7mm locomotive with it but it comes into its own for delicate weathering applications with minimal quantities of paint.

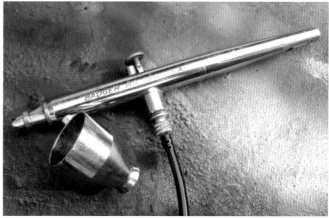

Above: This is the Badger 150, a standard modellers' airbrush used by Roy C. Link, Gordon Gravett, Iain Rice, Allan Sibley and many other leading modellers. I've had this one for 20 years – and it shows. The newer models have a series of V-notches set into the head, which allows air to escape when spraying close in and results in a cleaner line. The big colour cup, unfortunately, is not ideal when you only want to use tiny quantities of paint. Since I bought an Iwata I've relegated the Badger to more general work as it doesn't offer such fine control. It's great for scenic work though, as well as all-over livery applications.

Some may ask if an airbrush is really necessary, given the kind of effects that artist-modellers can achieve with conventional brushes alone. Only you can decide – all I can say is that an airbrush greatly simplifies the weathering process and accelerates it at the same time.

Air supply

A compressor is vital if you're going to use an airbrush with any frequency. It quickly repays its initial cost and the limitless supplies of (virtually) free air encourage experiment and refinement. You can buy a perfectly serviceable one for the price of a ready-to-run locomotive. In operation they can sometimes be a little noisy and in continuous use they may run hot – some have a thermal cut-out to cope with this. In these circumstances, a water trap is useful to prevent little spatters of condensation finding their way down the hose and onto your model.

Air delivery is normally adjustable by means of a pressure regulator, but with the more budget-priced designs this tends to be on the lines of a typical hotel shower – it's either one thing or the other, but it may be surprisingly tricky to reach that ideal in-between stage. About 25psi is about right for most weathering work. With a better compressor you can turn the air pressure right down for little wafts and spatters, or increase it for maximum saturation and paint atomisation (or for blasting dust out of the nooks and crannies on your model prior to painting). A pressure gauge, if accurate, is useful for checking that the compressor is delivering the pressure you want (that's with the airbrush attached, of course, rather than with an open hose), but your best indication is your own eyes. If the paint is going on the way you want it to go on, the reading doesn't matter.

Compressors with built-in reservoir tanks are useful but far from mandatory. They will kick in when the supply of air needs replenishing and trip out when pressure is built up. The advantages are a quiet operation and the evenness of air delivery, without pressure fluctuations; the downside is that they can be big, bulky and quite expensive. On a compressor without a tank there may be a tendency for the air supply to pulse, but to a degree this is ironed out by the pressure regulator that come as standard, these days, with most designs.

Modern compressors – as opposed to the kind of thing modellers acquire at car-boot sales, which probably come out of some old boy's garage and sound like a pre-war motorcycle – are very quiet in operation, with little vibration, and come complete with water trap, filter and adjustable pressure valve. Modeller-friendly compressors are advertised on internet sites at widely varying prices, so it pays to shop around. I've seen what appears to be the exact same compressor with different branding stickers at prices ranging from an eye-watering £210 down to considerably less than £50 on Amazon.

I find compressors are much of a muchness apart from the noise factor; one downside to using one for continuous spraying is that, sooner rather than later, you will get water condensing in the airline until it spits out all over the workpiece. Compressed air is very hot, containing moisture in vapour form. This passes through the water trap attached to the compressor – which is only a first line of defence, not a brick wall – and condenses in the hose. One suggested remedy involves fitting an extra-long hose between the compressor outlet and the filter/trap, with a second hose to the airbrush. In this way, the moisture cools off sufficiently to be separated out properly before reaching the outlet. My own solution is to stop spraying from time to time and let the compressor and airline cool down. Before resuming spraying, you can take the airbrush off the hose, switch on the compressor and blow out any water that's condensed inside.

You can also buy compressed air in cans. They work – up to a point – but this is an expensive way to power an airbrush and you have no control over the air pressure, which may decrease significantly as the can empties. This doesn't matter too much if you're firing off an air horn, but if you're working on a model then the paint may start to spatter because it's no longer fully atomised. However, I concede that cans may be useful if no power supply is immediately to hand, or if portability is essential.

My main objection to cans is that, if they're your only source of compressed air, you may well use half the available supply simply by cleaning the airbrush. As we'll see in a later section, keeping your airbrush clean by blowing fresh thinners through it at regular intervals is fundamental, but if you're buying cans then the temptation to skimp on cleaning is irresistible. A half-cleaned airbrush quickly becomes a blocked airbrush and you will lose even more of your precious air trying to clear it. Buy a compressor and be done with it. As well as encouraging you to try out new effects and techniques, you'll be better equipped to do a thorough cleaning job. If you still have half a locomotive to paint and your only can is three-quarters empty, you're not going to waste any more air than you have to on what you might well think of as non-productive cleaning. Thorough airbrush cleaning, unfortunately, is one of the most fruitful activities there is in this line of work.

This is my usual compressor, a 20-year-old Mini-Micon made by Badger. Despite the lack of maintenance and being lugged all over the place, it still functions perfectly well. If you have my book Modelling Diesels in 4mm Scale *(Hawksill Publishing, 1996) you can see the same compressor looking a great deal less careworn.*

This is the compressor with which I'll probably replace the Mini-Micon when it finally gives up the ghost – the Iwata Studio Series Sprint Jet. Professional painter Ian Rathbone tells me it's no use for blowing away dust and debris (and badly soldered parts) because you can't crank it up more than about 35psi, but I'm sure it'll be fine. It's marketed as virtually silent in operation but, when I had a go, I didn't think it was all that much quieter than the elderly Mini-Micon you can hear spluttering away in the background on my Weathering Techniques *DVD. Unless a bit of cloning has been going on, it seems to be available under various names and at varying prices.*

The studio

Whether or not I'm using an airbrush at the time, my preference for many years has been to carry out weathering outdoors, in the garden. On occasion I do work indoors under artificial light, a transition that is easily managed because I'm still using the same paints and the same techniques, even though the lighting is different.

I like to work outdoors in the sunlight because it's warm and no light source is anywhere near as good for our purposes as that generated by a complex fusion of gases millions of miles away. Indoors or out, most of my weathering is done sitting down with as much space as possible around me, so that I'm not tripping over air lines and power cables. You have to feel comfortable and there has to be no danger that the model will topple over while the paint is still wet. I like a high table – a working surface about 2ft 6in off the ground is fine, but 3ft would be perfect for me – because I get a good view of the sides of the model as well as the top. When I come to do the underpinnings – wheels, bogies, valve gear, etc – I can crouch or kneel down if I want to. A low table is no use because you're basically looking down on your work and have to tilt the model to get at the running gear. You can also weather standing up with the workpiece placed on a shelf at eye level, which I quite enjoy. If you're thinking of installing a permanent spray booth, this might be something to consider. The spray booths at Hobby Holidays are like this, so I know it works.

Painting turntable

I don't have an enormous *batérie de cuisine* when it comes to modelling tools, but my painting turntable is one of the most useful pieces of kit I possess. Mine is homemade, using a 'Lazy Susan' ballrace mechanism sandwiched by two lathe-turned discs of MDF. It enables me to swivel the workpiece around so I can work on it from any angle without having to touch the model, which is always a hazard when wet paint is about.

For 4mm scale work, something pizza-sized is ideal. For 7mm locomotives I park the model on a plank of wood that in turn sits centrally on the painting turntable. It seems stable enough – the only hazard is the risk of clouting something (an open can of paint is the favourite) as you spin the table round.

My painting turntable is one of the most useful tools I have. It enables me to spin the model around so I can weather it from all angles without physically touching it. Here I've been working on an HO scale GP7 – basically a Proto 2000 model with a chop nose and a lot of detail parts.

Similar items are available via the model trade, or you can buy a cake-icing turntable which will do the job just as well. Google, Amazon or eBay should bring up several options. My preference, based on past experience, is for something as solid and stable as possible.

Working conditions

As 99.9% of people have managed to work out, there is a huge difference between the kind of health and safety considerations endorsed by those in authority (i.e. who legislate on behalf of organisations that, in theory at any rate, may stand to lose large amounts of money if something goes badly wrong) and the kind of sensible, rational precautions that would be taken by anyone who values their health and well-being and doesn't always take what lawyers say too seriously.

To keep nanny-staters happy, you'd probably need to do your weathering in an isolation tank, wearing a space suit and breathing pure oxygen piped in from an external reservoir. You would need to sign a waiver stating that you understand what you're doing and accept the consequences. You would need to have a doctor and a team of lawyers on hand, along with risk assessors and other highly-paid professionals. Or you might just want to get on with your hobby.

Except for simple touching-up and titivation, I always use the airbrush outdoors so that the fumes readily dissipate downwind. I have a supply of simple face masks but I only use them on still days when the vapour hangs in the air, or when using cellulose-based paints (which is not very often and never in a weathering context). More sophisticated respirator masks are available from DIY stores, should you feel that you need one. I don't notice painters and decorators dressing up like Darth Vader.

If you do most of your work indoors, then I'd certainly endorse the acquisition or construction of a spray booth with an effective extraction system – in fact I'd go so far as to say it was pretty well essential, because you can't rely on the current of air running from an open door to an open window to keep you safe. Portable spray booths are available if you don't have the facility to have one permanently plumbed in. As generations of Missenden students will testify, working in a fug of paint fumes in a confined space is at best unpleasant and at worst has the potential to be extremely damaging to your health. It's a risk that's just not worth taking, so you will need to take responsibility for your own well-being and come up with a solution that's effective for you – which is why I choose to work outdoors with a gentle breeze behind me, rather than blundering around dressed like someone handling irradiated nuclear waste.

A portable spray booth is ideal if you don't have the space for a permanent setup. The trunking is simply hung out of the window where the nasties exhaust themselves to the atmosphere and harmlessly disperse. It's no more noisy than a fan heater.

Paint

T. S. Eliot measured out his life with coffee spoons. I've done it with tiny cans and bottles of model paint. Given that – compared with household emulsion and gloss – it's an extremely expensive way to buy paint, I dread to think how much I've spent on them over the last half-century and more, and how small an acreage I've actually covered.

I use ordinary Humbrol and Revell enamel paint for weathering. They are easy to find, they last a long time in the tin, the colours are exactly what I want and the paint surface dries fast enough to curb my impatience – but not so quickly that there isn't time to create lots of interesting after-effects before it finally cures.

Others speak highly of acrylic paints. While I do use them in certain modelling applications (such as putting on basic liveries), I find they dry far too quickly and are less malleable than enamels used in similar circumstances. There's less time in which to play around with them – subtle colour-blending seems particularly difficult – or to correct errors.

To let the paint down to the appropriate consistency, I use ordinary household white spirit or turps substitute. All thinners are basically distilled crude and I see

This range of ultra high-quality weathering paints is marketed by leading airbrush manufacturer Iwata under the Real Deal banner. The acrylic colours are specially formulated for airbrushing but conventional brush-painting is perfectly feasible. The pigment is very fine, more akin to a filter, allowing you to build up incredibly subtle effects through multiple applications. While they carry specific-sounding names such as Old Oil, Dark Rust and Fertile Soil, a little experimentation is clearly the name of the game.

This is the minimalist palette from which all the airbrush-weathered effects in this book were created – Matt Leather (Humbrol No 62) and Gunmetal No 27004 from Humbrol's Metalcote range, as well as any old Matt Black and Matt White (Revell in this case).

I use straight DIY-store white spirit as a thinner for enamel paint and also for general cleaning up. Cellulose thinners – which should never go anywhere near a plastic model – are very good for purging airbrushes at the end of a spraying session. I make sparing use of airbrush thinners, not for their intended purpose but as a solvent with various other materials – acrylic weathering filters, powder pigment and gouache.

no point in paying 10 or 20 times as much, measured by volume, for a branded product labelled as a thinners specially formulated for airbrushes or any other modelling application. Maybe others can see the difference, but I can't – although I sense that the proprietary brands evaporate faster and thus the paint is dry to the touch in a shorter timespan. If you're stuck, lighter fluid (with the usual safety provisos: it has a low flashpoint and its fumes are toxic) does the trick, but since the world collectively gave up smoking this may not be easy to find around the house.

For weathering with the Badger or Iwata, I normally let down the enamel paint approximately 50:50 with thinners to about the consistency of full-cream milk. Give it a good stir – a minute or more – and then stir it again for the same length of time. If your paint isn't well blended, little globules are guaranteed to block up the capillary tubes inside your airbrush and you will have to stop work and strip the brush right down to clear them out. This will take a lot longer than two minutes and leave you feeling very frustrated.

A greater dilution of paint may be useful in certain applications or when using a very fine airbrush. With a bigger airbrush – or when using the Badger with its heavy-duty head – I will use a proportionally thicker paint mix, maybe three parts of paint to one of thinner. Different airbrushes seem to prefer subtly different paint mixes – my Iwata likes a slightly thinner paint than the Badger – so some measure of trial and error is called for until you find the optimum proportions. Adjustment is easy – if the paint is clearly coming out too thick, then add a few drops of thinner before it clogs up altogether. If it's too thin, then add a brushful or two of paint.

Modellers often seem worried that the paint they apply in creating weathering effects will build up to such a depth that it starts to obscure the detail on their models. This certainly can happen if you apply paint straight from the can with a six-inch distemper brush, but a layer of airbrushed weathering paint applied in the way I do it is barely a few atoms thick. To prove my point, I broke off a piece of the dried paint that has built up like a crust on the surface of my painting turntable. I've been using this turntable week in, week out for the best part of 15 years and the thickness of the paint layer, measured with a micrometer, is a whisper under 20 thou' (0.0020in, which works out at about 0.5mm or, in old money, 1/50th of an inch). That wafer-thin encrustation must represent many hundreds of individual paint layers; if they cumulatively add up to something no thicker than a business card, it ought to give you some idea of the minimal thickness of a typical paint application using an airbrush.

Something I've come to relatively recently is the use of gouache (artists' watercolours) in weathering. This is a lot less straightforward to use than airbrushed enamels, so perhaps it should come under the category of 'advanced weathering'. We'll look at gouache in the step-by-step sequence in Chapter 6 where I weather a Class 56.

Bottom: Artists' gouache is endorsed by leading US modellers for its delicacy and endless mutability – if you don't like an effect, you can delete it and go back to the previous stage. As a method, I find it slow-going but extremely satisfying. Later on, I'll describe weathering the bodywork of a Class 56 using gouache.

Weathering sprays

These are available in aerosol form from various sources, such as Railmatch (enamel paint), Games Workshop (acrylic) and Modelmates (water-soluble translucent inks). Whatever the differences in their composition, they work in a similar way – you

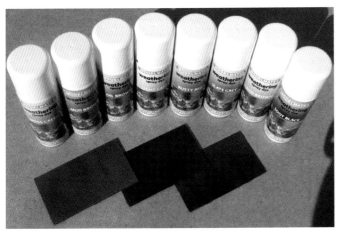

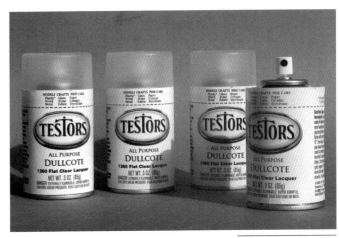

A range of ink-based weathering sprays from Modelmates. Translucent and water soluble, they can be worked on for up to 10 minutes after spraying. Gentle stroking with a damp brush or tissue can create some surprisingly subtle effects – the ink can be wiped or dabbed to create a patchy surface, encouraging it to collect in nooks and crannies. The main drawback is the sheen that builds up, which can be countered with Testor's Dullcote or a similar matting agent.

basically spray them on and then, if you feel so inclined, immediately wipe some or most of the pigment off to produce a blotchy or streaked look.

Even the acrylics can be worked on for up to 10 minutes after spraying. Gentle stroking with a damp brush or tissue can create some surprisingly subtle effects, most effective on textured surfaces – the pigment can be wiped or dabbed to create a patchy finish, encouraging it to collect in nooks and crannies. Multiple passes with different shades produce interesting results and any faint sheen that builds up can be countered with a good matt finish such as Testor's Dullcote.

I've enjoyed using weathering sprays in scenic work where a saturation approach is called for, but when it comes to locomotives – especially in the smaller scales – they lack any subtlety. With an aerosol you have very little control over delivery or direction, and it's all too easy to get paint everywhere. You can work round this on coaching stock and multiple-units by masking the sides before spraying the roofs and underframes with the appropriate ready-mixed colours, but I'm not sure how effective this would be on a locomotive. To achieve results that compare with what can be achieved via an airbrush or careful hand-brushing calls for remarkable skills. If you already have such ability, I really can't imagine why you'd be playing around with aerosols.

Powders

Weathering powders are a very useful way of embellishing effects primarily achieved with paint. I think of them as spices or condiments added to the main dish, but not as a meal in themselves. Which is not to say that you can't create effective weathering using powders alone, merely that I feel it's not the ideal way to do it. All too often, powder-weathered models look like . . . well, powder-weathered models rather than accurate impressions of the real thing.

Weathering powders – Carr's and MIG are probably the best-known brands in the UK – consist of tiny particles of coloured pigment with a greasy consistency that enables them to cling to the surface of the model. They work best on uneven or textured finishes, where they collect in the little nooks and crannies. On a smooth, high-gloss surface there's nothing for them to latch onto, so they quickly fall off and are therefore useless for weathering.

I use a variety of tools for applying weathering powders, from kids' paintbrushes (no point in ruining your best sables) to cotton buds and even scraps of styrene foam, anything that will make a mark and look natural. As far as application technique is concerned, we're talking about stabbing or dabbing

Testor's Dullcote is the only aerosol matting agent that works for me. It's an American product – UK suppliers can be located with a bit of Googling but, because availability may be limited, bulk buying is a good idea. I primarily use this clear, flat lacquer to seal powders and water-soluble paints such as gouache, but it's better than any matt varnish at giving a dead-flat finish to a model.

Carr's weathering powders have been around for quite a few years now. I use some colours more than others – the greens are great on buildings, where they immediately suggest the effects of a British climate – but they can be mixed with one another to create interesting effects. Experimentation often results in unexpected outcomes.

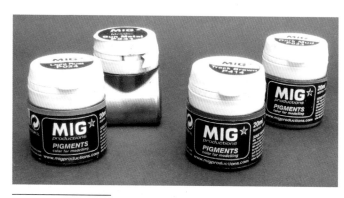

MIG powders are very popular with military modellers. They are formulated with weathering very much in mind and are correspondingly fine-textured. The names of the colours – Track Brown, Light Rust – shouldn't be any barrier to improvisation.

actions rather than dainty watercolour brushstrokes. People often ask whether they should varnish surfaces to protect the powders but I don't see much point, since the coating will immediately alter the colour effects you've worked so hard to achieve.

Other materials can be used in a similar way to weathering powders. Pastel chalks from artists' suppliers are a very economical way of building up subtle weathering effects – they come in stick form so you can scrape off a small quantity with a scalpel blade, either applying it to the model neat or blending it with other pastel colours. Unsurprisingly, particles of real soot, rust and ash (cigarette ash is particularly fine) can be very effective as weathering agents. I'm also told fingerprint powder is as good as it gets in achieving a light dusting and discoloration on a painted surface – unfortunately, it's extremely expensive, being such a specialised product, and enquiries among chums employed by HM Constabulary have failed to yield any free samples.

Weathering solutions

These are rather like weathering powders in liquid form – a fine silt held in suspension in what I assume is isopropyl alcohol. After giving the contents of the bottle a good stir, brush a small quantity on your model and allow it to find its own way around. The carrying solution evaporates and you're left with a subtle application of weathering that settles in nooks and crannies.

The best-known products in this area are probably the Rustall range of weathering solutions from the USA. There are several products in the range, all of which have their uses, working equally effectively on metal, plastic, resin and even card. Rustall itself is a patented product that contains real rust and is designed to give the impression of random corrosion. First you let the fluid flow onto the item that is to be 'rusted'; the initial application leaves only a modest amount of rusting but, after allowing it to dry, you can build up successive layers through repeat applications. This allows you to control the amount of weathering you apply to your locomotive, from a modest film of rust through to a total Barry scrapyard look.

Blackwash is a similar kind of product that will darken and bring out detail and texture around panel lines, bolts, hatches and other fine detail, thus throwing them into sharp relief. Because it tends to stay put rather than run everywhere – the effect of surface tension, I assume – it's useful in local applications as an alternative to dabbing on much-diluted enamel paint, which tends to wander.

The Rustall range contains many of those oh-so-subtle American products that, with patience, can be used to create some stunning effects. I'm particularly fond of running in Blackwash – labelled '2' in this view – as a way of emphasising panel lines.

As with Rustall, Blackwash looks very understated at first but it's easy to build up the effect with repeat applications.

The other main products are Deadflat, a coating designed to create a random flat finish, and Dust, which is exactly that – a fine dirt from the hills of Mendoncino County in California. In constitution, it is a clay silt that is ground and sifted into a fine, talcum-like dust that works brilliantly – and far more subtly than most weathering powders – to lighten local areas. After application you can coat it with Rustall to achieve a very convincing effect of corrosion and flaking. There's also Weatherall, which is useful for achieving the effect of well-weathered wood which is not really part of the locomotive brief, other than as potential experimentation.

Paintbrushes

Modellers tend to be hard on their paintbrushes, probably because we try to put them to uses they're not really intended for. We need the delicacy of a watercolour brush with the durability of one designed for oils. Good quality sable brushes, properly looked after, will last for some while but, as these become increasingly difficult (and expensive) to obtain, alternatives have to be considered.

Fortunately, choosing paintbrushes for weathering applications is very much a case of horses for courses. For weathering powders and general slosh I use nothing grander than cheap children's paintbrushes. They rarely cost much but it's worth looking out some good ones and buying in quantity. The kind of kids' brushes you find in your local newsagents will fall to bits after you've used them a couple of times.

In the sense of using brushes to lay on paint as smoothly and evenly as possible, I do very little brush painting in my kind of weathering. I do, however, routinely use brushes to move airbrush-applied paint around, which is a different thing entirely. Sometimes you can just flail away with your eyes closed, but where control and delicacy are critical I always push the boat out and buy the best. For years this meant top-quality sables, especially in sizes 0-2, and a half-inch flattie brush is also essential. Until recently, synthetic brushes never failed to disappoint (they just don't like enamel paint), but nowadays I get on very well with the blue-handled Aquafine range from Daler-Rowney. They keep their shape despite the hammering I give them and last an awful lot longer than other synthetic artists' brushes.

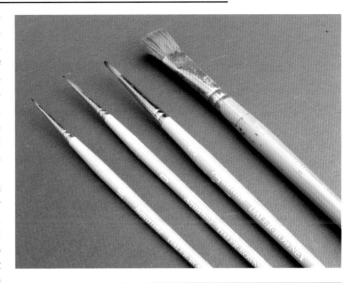

For many years I used high-quality sable brushes, which are increasingly costly and hard to find. In the wake of a number of random and generally unsatisfactory experiments with synthetic brushes – they lost their shape too quickly, the bristles fell out and the ferrules worked loose – I arrived with considerable relief at the Aquafine range from Daler-Rowney (locate your nearest supplier at www.daler-rowney.com). They are tough and good at putting on delicate brushstrokes. They're also remarkably inexpensive – about £3.50 for a general-purpose No 1 or 2 round (candle-flame) brush, and £5.50 for a big flattie. More to the point, they do the business remarkably well and seem to last a lot longer in good working order than the other synthetic brushes I've tried, especially those cheap and nasty things sold in model shops.

I don't know exactly what the Aquafine bristles are made from – Daler-Rowney's website speaks mysteriously of 'dark-tipped sable-like filaments' – but they seem to withstand enamel paint pretty well. The lady at my local artist's supply shop is equally enthusiastic about their suitability for acrylics, though this is an unknown quantity to me. Thus far I haven't tried the very small brushes in the range or the more specialised shapes, but I've been very pleased with the round and flat brushes that ubiquitous in model-painting. As they age, most of my paintbrushes traditionally tend to be relegated in turn to rough weathering, paint stirring and finally the bin, but these Aquafines seem to remain in pretty good shape with no more advanced a care regime than a thorough wash in clean white spirit at the end of each session. Even if paint is inadvertently left to harden, a dunk in cellulose thinners and a bit of careful persuasion will soon restored the brush to life.

Once a brush is past its best, however, there's no point trying to persuade it to do something it's no longer fit for – but it can still be useful. You can't paint a straight line with its straggly, paint-clogged bristles but you can use it to add 'random' marks such as scrapes, abrasions and other visible wounds, dabbed on with neat paint. Ironically perhaps, you'll find it a lot harder to create these effects with a brand-new sable.

And when – even by my standards – brushes are utterly clapped out, they become paint-stirrers. Stirring thick paint with your best sables, wiping the excess on kitchen roll and giving them a good clean will dramatically shorten their working lives. It may keep your local artists' supply shop in business, but it's not good practice.

Improvised applicators

As we will see when we come to look at our worked examples, weathering applied by airbrush alone can often create a surface finish that is far too smooth and regular. This blemish-free surface is what the airbrush was originally developed for, effortlessly improving the complexions of film stars in 10x8 glossies. Real weathering, however, can be distinctly uneven in patches. This is where we have to put the airbrush down and think of other ways of applying colour.

There is nothing modellers do that has not already been done before in other media, so it's well worth your while seeing how others do it. Pukka artists (the people who drink absinthe, wear berets and have colourful personal lives) work paint by various means besides brushes; indeed some painters barely use brushes at all.

Their batérie de cuisine includes accepted tools such as palette knives as well as improvised devices of many kinds – from fingers and pointed sticks to old rags and broken bricks, anything that will make a mark.

For the model maker, the scope is as wide as your imagination in representing irregular marks and patterns. Sometimes I will scratch or abrade paint to produce a particular effect, whether by simply scoring the surface or breaking through to the colour beneath. For this I'll use anything from a blunt scalpel blade to a wooden cocktail stick or emery board.

To create a spattering effect I will spray water (from a plant mister) over the base coat and then airbrush a different colour over the droplets. When they evaporate, they leave a mottled patch where the underpainting has been masked. Odd bits of expanded polystyrene and other kinds of foam are good for irregular dabbing or stippling effects, especially where a suggestion of texture such as that found on a well-rusted surface is required. Different sizes and grades produce different effects – this is where clapped-out paintbrushes can enjoy a final burst of glory. In use, simply dip or coat whatever you're using in paint or powder and apply to the model with a wiping, dabbing or scouring action.

Sponge wedges from the makeup counter are also very useful in weathering applications where a smudgy randomness is desirable.

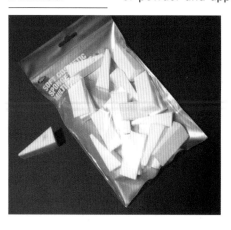

Remember that you can always modulate or even remove the effect by airbrushing over the top.

Makeup brushes (they come in all shapes and sizes) are very good for gently caressing powders already applied, encouraging them to blend and integrate into what has gone before. Putting paint or powder on a model is rarely a complete action in itself, but forms part of a chain. That initial spot of rust on a smokebox may, by the time you've finished the project, look radically different – and this may not always be by design. Accidental and fortuitous discoveries have a great part to play in developing your weathering techniques, and so does a willingness to improvise. This is certainly what keeps it fresh for me, almost 50 years after I first weathered a Hornby-Dublo locomotive.

A woman applying makeup is a bit like a modeller applying weathering. You seek something less than overall saturation coverage; you want colours to merge subtly; you need a degree of translucency. Dusting, smudging and highlighting all come into the equation. I long ago realised that makeup brushes of different kinds – acquired from an assortment of wives, girlfriends and mistresses – could have many uses once they were spirited away from the dressing table.

This is the kind of effect you can only recreate with a high-quality airbrush – the heavily corroded silencer on a GBRf class 66. Budget-priced models are just not up to this degree of subtlety – complicated and time-consuming masking techniques would have been necessary to achieve a similar effect.

Match a good airbrush with mastery of hand-finishing techniques and you're onto a winner. Here a FIA Trains model of one of the ex-LMS Co-Cos gets the treatment. The gentle modulations of airbrush-applied weathering have been broken up by careful brushwork to create prototypical streaking effects, suggesting leakage from the engine room.

Below: At the heart of my weathering methods are just two paint colours that can be mixed together to create seemingly endless permutations of tone. One is Matt Leather (Humbrol No 62), which looks nothing like leather or anything else in the natural world. The other is the astonishing Gunmetal, No 27004 from Humbrol's Metalcote range, which can be used as a straight (and very dead) matt black. However, there are metallic particles floating in suspension in the paint; if, when dry, it is gently polished with a cotton bud or fingertip then the particles come to life to give a hugely convincing metal sheen. Having long been afraid that these paints might one day be deleted from the Humbrol catalogue, I prefer to buy in quantity.

Above: *The beleaguered remains of an Athearn GP60, cannibalised for kitbash projects and used here to road-test a new range of weathering products on behalf of the manufacturer. The experimental colours arrived in nail-varnish bottles!*

Above: *A digital camera is a priceless tool, not just for recording weathering effects but also for photographing work in progress. Models that look fine in the flesh show all kinds of shortcomings when studied onscreen. In the latter stages of painting I like to view images in black and white, to see if I've got the tones right when set against similar shots in 50-year-old magazines.*

Below: *Your eyes and your powers of observation are the most valuable tools of all, but sometimes you have no option but to use your imagination. The magnificent Great Eastern Decapod came and went decades before I was born so when I built this P4 model I had to try and visualise what kind of external condition it was kept in. As far as I know there are no photographs of this experimental locomotive at work or even in steam.*

The Practicalities

Weathering a locomotive is not the St Valentine's Day Massacre. You don't blaze away with an airbrush like it's a machinegun. You work away carefully. Every move you make should be considered. Use the minimum amount of paint or powder necessary to do the job effectively (the 'single bullet' strategy). Restraint is the keynote. Understatement is everything. Overkill is bad news (although it can be redeemable).

At the same time, weathering can be (and should be) enormous fun. Once you get the hang of it, it becomes a continuously flowing operation but with a clearly defined beginning and end. Having practised the art for a long time now, I can say that the ideal way to arrive at this happy state is to understand what you're trying to achieve and what might be the best way to go about it.

Not everyone has a delicate touch, that's for sure. I have taught enough people the essentials of weathering technique to be able to tell that some have a natural aptitude for this kind of thing, while others will just have to learn the hard way – which means a great deal of practice and a lot of self-criticism.

I have mixed feelings about weathering models in batches. As far as coaches and units go, it's probably the only way to do it – take a complete rake, start at one end and work right through to the tail lamp, introducing a few subtle variations along the way. With locomotives it's different. I prefer to think of each one as an individual project and weather it accordingly, otherwise you end up with a group that look pretty much the same. Using similar materials and paint shades will automatically give you consistency, but by weathering them at different times and using a range of different – but complimentary – techniques you will achieve the necessary variety. When I was working on this group of HO scale EMD diesels, it was actually quite hard to avoid repetition. American units normally run in multiple consists or lash-ups and while the same engines can be MU'd together for months at a time, they still retain a clear individuality in terms of external appearance.

No one is automatically disqualified either. Weathering a model locomotive is not portrait painting – believe me, all of us can do it if we put our minds to it and work through some all-too-familiar negative misconceptions: 'I don't have a top-quality airbrush.' 'I'm afraid I'll make a mess of it.' 'I tried it once and it was a disaster.' 'What do I do if it all goes wrong?'

Lack of confidence and fear of failure are as big a deterrent as lack of experience – perhaps they're the same thing. However, anyone who can build a kit or wire up a turnout ought to be able to successfully weather a locomotive, whereas those who are just plain clumsy (but bash ahead regardless) are likely to make a complete mess of it unless given some very specific guidance. Some of the greatest satisfaction at my weekend courses comes from seeing people who regarded themselves as total duffers learn, eventually, that they have what it takes.

It's the same as playing a musical instrument – what may seem like a wild improvisation is, for the musician, quite a controlled (and controlling) experience. Making a model come to life before your eyes can be an exciting process, but you need to be calm and considered about everything you do. Frame of mind is an important factor, since you're not going to produce your best work if you're in a filthy mood or have just been chased round the garden by a 30-foot crocodile. Relax; get yourself comfortable; make sure you have everything to hand and tell yourself you're going to enjoy the next hour or so. You may be pleasantly surprised by the outcome.

If you're of a nervous disposition, I suggest you first explore the basics of weathering on something that doesn't matter. Spend an hour or two throwing paint or powder at any old junk you can find in a kitchen drawer or at the back of the garage. (An impromptu rummage has just brought to light a selection of plastic cutlery, some industrial-scale nuts and bolts, any number of 35mm film canisters and assorted offcuts of hardboard, all of which would be ideal for practice sessions.) Set them up and spray paint at them to see what happens. Spray from different distances – a foot away, six inches, one inch – and observe the results. As you come in close and point the airbrush at one particular spot, you'll notice how quickly paint builds up and starts to run; in future, therefore, remember to keep the airbrush moving. When you spray from a distance, you'll observe how thin and gritty the coverage appears at first and why it may be necessary to repeat some of the coats. You'll see, too, that spraying a flat surface is a lot easier than painting a round object, as well as observing lots of other entry-level facts.

When you're done and you feel you've begun to get the hang of things – or have just become bored with painting jam-jar lids – chuck your practice objects away and have a rummage in your kit cupboard. A few old, busted plastic kits or a spare locomotive body would be ideal – it doesn't matter if half the bits have fallen off, what we want is something that looks more like a railway engine than a plastic clothes peg. Set up whatever you've found and have a go at it. There's no need to use specific weathering colours – the more startling the contrast in the shades that you use, the better you'll be able to see the effects.

Using the airbrush

Holding an airbrush is no more difficult than using a knife and fork – it's not like trying to eat with chopsticks while wearing boxing gloves. The key thing is that it feels comfortable in your hand. I hold mine exactly as I hold a pen, as do most people, but I had one student who – having tried using his index finger to operate the trigger – felt a lot easier holding the airbrush in his upturned palm like a screwdriver or a chisel, with his thumb on the release.

Whatever grip you use, it will soon start to feel like the most natural thing in the world. However, you still need to concentrate on what you're doing to avoid getting into bad habits. As a case in point, a lot of airbrush weathering involves moving along the model, keeping a constant distance between the paint tip and your loco. Surprisingly perhaps, you don't use the wonderfully flexible joint that is your wrist to make a pass with your airbrush. Instead, you hold your

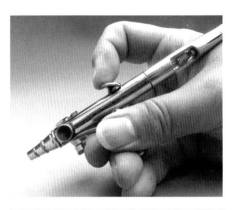

The airbrush is sitting comfortably in my right hand. The business end is balanced on the knuckle of my second finger while the tail of the airbrush rests on the fleshy pad between my thumb and index finger. Everything is controlled by my index finger.

I press down very gently with my index finger to release the air. The actual degree of travel in the trigger is very slight but it gives you all the control you need, from the gentlest of wafts to full pressure. Pulling the trigger back at the same time as you press down releases the paint flow. Again, the movement is slight but the degree of control is remarkable.

I've pulled the trigger right back for maximum paint flow. I don't often do this, at least while weathering.

wrist fairly rigidly and move your arm instead, flexing as necessary with your elbow and shoulder. This is because you need to keep a consistent distance between the workpiece and the airbrush – if you move your wrist in an arc, the spraying distance will change and it'll makes a considerable difference to the paint coverage you achieve.

The only time you move the airbrush in a curve is when you're following the outline of, say, a boiler or a cab roof, where you need to keep a constant distance from your work to ensure an even coverage. Unfortunately, flexing of the wrist is more suited to concave surfaces than the convex curves that prevail in modelling, so in this situation you'll need to keep your wrist rigid and use your forearm to do the work.

How far away do you spray from? Generally speaking, with a decent airbrush you can come as close as you like. I add general weathering from no more than three or four inches away, while specific effects are created with airbrush an inch or less from the model. Beginners seem to expect that you should spray from at least a foot away (though I'm not sure why), but all this does is create a grainy, gritty effect because the paint is almost dry on contact with the model.

My approach involves spraying small amounts of paint from close range rather than blasting it in from afar. This head-on shot shows the kind of distance I work from, but if you have a more modest airbrush you may need to pull back slightly.

Most of your weathering will inevitably be done from above the model, which is also the angle from which we normally view them.

The better you can coordinate the release of air and paint, the more control you have and the closer you will be able to work. Cruder airbrushes don't offer this kind of delicacy and there are physical limits to how close up you can get (you'll have to find out for yourself) or how well you can control the paint application. An airbrush that just blasts away like a flame-thrower will not be a lot of use, I'm afraid.

Right-handers generally spray left to right, left-handers the other way round. The key thing here is that you don't point your airbrush directly at the model and press the trigger. Aim instead at a point a few inches to the left or right of the model, begin to swing your arm and then release the trigger so that the mix of paint and air is already flowing by the time it makes contact with the workpiece. Any spits and spats of poorly-mixed paint tend to shoot out the second that you press the trigger, before settling down to a steady flow. Starting to spray with the airbrush pointing away from the model minimises the risk of these blebs becoming a nuisance.

Move slowly across the model at the rate of an inch a second or so, keeping parallel. Allow a measure of overrun before releasing the trigger when you get to the other side. To achieve a wider spray pattern or increase the level of coverage, go back to the starting point and make another circuit. With most weathering effects, however, a single pass is sufficient.

Subtler weathering applications – including the blending and building-up of colours – are more local, spraying one small area at a time. If you're worried about overspray, use a simple card mask to stop paint spreading to where you don't want it to go. This is particularly relevant if you have only a simple airbrush that does not offer fine control of paint delivery. As before, get the air/paint mixture flowing and quickly move the airbrush to spray the desired area. With practice, it's quite easy to hold back the paint until the airbrush is pointing where you want the paint to go.

However, you do need to get more-or-less level with the model to paint areas such as the tank sides, as here, or the chassis. A low-angle or eye-level viewpoint will quickly reveal the bald patches you missed because you were spraying from a helicopter.

Coming in really close this time to spray the top of the running plate under the tank. Again, there is very little paint and just enough air to do the job. If I gave it full pelt from this kind of range, paint would flood the model and the effect would be ruined.

Work in progress

Airbrush weathering is a balancing act between hand and eye. The physical mechanics of it can usually take care of themselves, but you need to be aware of what you're doing.

One of the first things you'll learn is that colours dry quite a bit lighter compared with how they look when wet. Fortunately, you can judge the effect almost immediately. Within a minute or less of the paint going on, it visibly starts to dry as the solvent evaporates. The darkness of the wet paint miraculously disappears and the pigments settle down to an approximation of their final appearance. The white spirit I use is quite slow to evaporate in comparison to some of the thinners on the market; if this is a problem to you, you can experiment with different types.

Enamel paint takes a lot longer to dry properly than you may imagine, though we can turn this to our advantage as we will see in some of our worked examples. It will only be 'wet' for a matter of minutes, remaining workable for around an hour, but it will be days before it has finally set hard. While the chemical reaction is taking place, the risk of getting fingerprints and smudges on the model is considerable. Dust in the atmosphere is not a problem but stray sleeves and elbows can do an awful lot of damage to a part-painted model.

During the weathering process I avoid touching the model as far as possible. If you really must move it – and I warn you that even the most experienced of us can knock things over – then handle it by the buffers with your fingers as pressure pads, or use a part of the model that has not yet been painted.

It's best that the model stays put and that you do the moving. This is where a painting turntable (see page 48) is invaluable – you can spin it round to work on whatever part of the model needs your attention. In our worked examples in the next section, you'll see that it's virtually impossible to get by without such a device. Trying to work around the model usually involves tangled air hoses; if you put it on, say, a piece of wood so that you can move it around, there's always the risk that it will topple over.

To put the basic livery on a locomotive you need to forget that it has a top, a bottom, two sides and two ends – in order to achieve an even paint coverage you have to think of it as a three-dimensional shape that you approach from all points of the compass, not just from a few inches above the boiler or roof. To ensure the paint goes on uniformly, I usually spray bodyshells when they're hanging from the clothes line, stand them on end on the painting turntable or even lay them flat on their backs.

Weathering is different, however, as you don't normally need to weather the underside of a model. At the same time, it's tempting to spray everything from a position just slightly above the locomotive but this will leave bald patches on, say, the bottom half of the boiler or the bodyside turnunder of a Class 37. At some stage in the process, you'll need to spray from a position level with or even slightly below the model. You can do this either by kneeling or by placing the locomotive on blocks to raise it up to eye level. If you're careful, you can grip the model by the buffers and tilt it back to apply paint to the wheels, brake gear, lower firebox, tender or bogie frames and other hard-to-reach areas. You can overspray with different shades ands tones as soon as you're ready but, because the paint is still soft beneath an outer skin that's only atoms thin, you need to be extra careful not to damage the paint you've already applied.

So how much paint do you put on? I would say just enough to do the job. For a start, you'll almost certainly want some of the original livery colour to show through, which means applying only light coats of weathering – more of a mist than a downpour. What you don't want is a model covered from head to toe in a 100% solid application of Pro Paints Plus Authentic Loco Dirt. Instead, you can build up the effects gradually, first spraying on a base colour (generally a warm dark grey with a distinct brownish tinge) without either putting it on too evenly or worrying too much about leaving some areas virtually untouched. Then you can add a lighter version of the same colour, concentrating particularly on any areas you may have missed; if necessary, you can also add a third, darker version of the weathering mix. I find three subtly varied applications of the same basic shade are generally sufficient – any more and the effect becomes curiously muddied.

It's important to evaluate your work as you go along. My weathering normally takes place in a creative blur, but I do pause from time to time to look at where I've got to and where I need to go. Be honest with yourself and consider what you see. This is where my minimum-quantities approach pays off, because it is very much easier to add more than to take off any excess. A gap of a few minutes gives you a fresh perspective on what's been achieved so far – take a digital photograph of your model and view it on-screen, which is a never-failing way of finding out what looks good so far and what doesn't. Better still, once the basic weathering has been applied and the paintshop finish has (for the most part) been superficially obscured, I suggest taking a break for an hour or so – when you come back, the next stage will probably be obvious to you.

If you feel things have not been going well and are worried you may be heading for disaster, I'd suggest a break is even more of a good idea. I'm not talking about abandoning the work for good, merely getting a little space between yourself and your model. Once things have calmed down, I usually find it's not anywhere near as bad as I'd thought – a remedial waft or two of paint to cover up something in the wrong colour or wrong place (or both) should put things right. Despite all my caution, I often overdo it with the weathering powders and expect to have to do a bit of overpainting to tone them down into acceptability. But don't panic and try to paint your way out of trouble – if you can't see when enough is enough, you'll end up with weathering overkill.

Very rarely have I had to go back to square one and start all over again. People seem very anxious about the permanence of the weathering materials they plan to use, in case they can't get them off again; if you adopt a cautious one-step-at-a-time approach, rather than saturation bombing your loco, this shouldn't happen. If all else fails and you really do have a disaster on your hands, use a liberal amount of thinners to get as much of the offending paint off as possible. This is best done immediately but, since it takes at least a day for enamel paint to harden beyond workability, you still have an hour or two of leeway before reaching for the paint stripper.

Cleaning your airbrush

Achieving this kind of weathered finish, on an otherwise out-of-the-box Hornby model, depends to a great extent on keeping your airbrush in tip-top condition. If it is not, it will spit and snarl and it may eventually gum itself up completely. This is a penance easily avoided.

Cleanliness is next to godliness where airbrushes are concerned. Introducing a rigorous maintenance programme is the best way to get the most from your airbrush. In terms of performance, one of the most important – and also most neglected – aspects of using an airbrush is to keep the damned thing clean. Using an airbrush should be as easy as picking up a pen, but this isn't always the case – possibly because, while painting a model is exciting, cleaning an airbrush with the necessary degree of thoroughness is just plain boring.

In the past, whenever I bought a new airbrush, I'd be amazed at how much better it performed than my old one. Within weeks the differences had started to even out, and it took me a long time to realise that this wasn't just because the euphoria was wearing off. It was more the case that deposits of dried paint were beginning to build up inside the airbrush; I wasn't cleaning it properly and this affected its ability to function well. The paint flow became intermittent and I no longer seemed to have such fine control. The airbrush would spit and snarl, depositing undigested blobs

of paint where I least wanted them. Sometimes the performance was so inhibited that I'd have to stop work and blast neat thinners through the airbrush in a bid to smooth out the paint delivery. In other words, most of the advantages of owning a better airbrush were cancelled out because I wasn't looking after it as well as I should.

I can now say with some assurance that the best way to upgrade your airbrush to match the performance of a model at least 150% dearer is to give it a really thorough cleaning. On the other hand, you can make your top-of-the-range Iwata behave like something from a pound shop by neglecting this all-important aspect of airbrushing.

Unfortunately, clogged or partially blocked airbrushes are no use to anyone and most of the difficulties associated with them come down to poor standards of cleanliness. The top two complaints seem to involve the needle becoming immobilised because paint build-up has caused the internal clearances to seize up, or the paint tip becoming blocked up with hardened paint so that nothing can get through.

For an airbrush to work properly, the gap between the point of the needle and the inside face of the paint tip must be immeasurable – a couple of thousandths of an inch, if that. Water and thinners can get through but anything more viscous than milk will cause it to choke. As a consequence, even a blob of inadequately stirred paint will clog it up and warm compressed air, blowing over a film of paint at 25psi or so, will harden it off almost as effectively as a hairdryer.

Airbrushes are quite easy to keep in good working order and so these problems can be mitigated, if not avoided entirely. The first thing is to establish a cleaning regime and to stick to it rigidly. This kicks in even before I use my airbrush, especially if it hasn't been out of its case for some time. I'll withdraw the needle and gently clean the tip with a tissue moistened by thinners. Sometimes, even though it's been thoroughly cleaned before putting it away, a little residual paint will have seeped through the plumbing and collected around the paint tip and/or the main bearing – you can tell this has

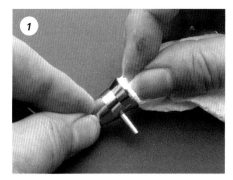

1: After using the airbrush, take off the colour cup and, with a piece of kitchen roll soaked in thinners, wipe out all the accumulated paint from the inside.

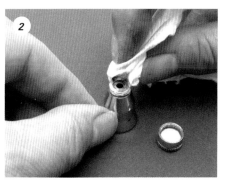

2: Some colour cups (this one is from an Iwata airbrush) can be further dismantled, so you can reach those otherwise inaccessible areas where paint accumulates.

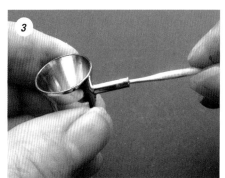

3: Sharpen a wooden cocktail stick to use as a type of reamer to get paint out of the internal passages of the colour cup. This works best if you have previously soaked the cup in cellulose thinners. Use soft brass wire to remove stubborn build-ups.

4: When it's thoroughly clean, refit the colour cup to the airbrush and spray several cupfuls of clean thinners through it. Repeat the process until the fluid flows clear.

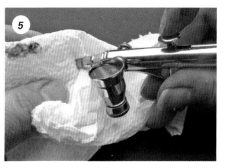

5: You can speed this process by backwashing the airbrush. Put your finger over the tip of the airbrush so that air is forced back down the system and into the colour cup. Bubbles will form and the thinners will quickly discolour on account of all the paint residues being blown back.

6: The head assembly can now be removed – some airbrushes have a special tool for this – to expose the delicate paint tip and the business end of the needle. Be very careful when handling an airbrush in such a state of undress.

7: Very gently remove the needle from the airbrush. On some makes, such as the Badger, you need to keep the brush right way up otherwise the trigger assembly will fall out. They are swine to refit.

8: Even after a good sluicing out it's surprising how much paint still remains, although by now it will be well watered down. If you had merely blown a few cupfuls of thinners through the airbrush and left it at that, this stuff would be drawn by capillary action into the paint tip, where it would harden and quite possibly block the airbrush.

9: Wipe the needle clean on a piece of kitchen roll. You often get quite a build-up where the needle passes through the Teflon bearing or tube that separates the paint chamber from the trigger assembly, a couple of inches back from the tip. This may need gentle abrasion to remove.

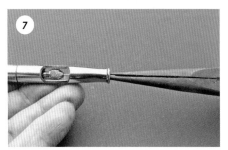

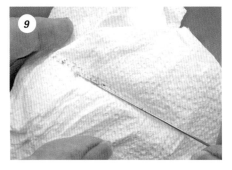

happened because you'll need to give the needle a gentle tug to pull it free.

Having cleaned and refitted the needle, I'll now spray some neat thinners (white spirit) through the airbrush – it's surprising how often a hint of the previous colour remains, even though you may have thought you'd cleaned it thoroughly. This is because the solvent will have evaporated over time but a few residual grains of paint will still remain.

Only now is the airbrush ready for use and you will still need to be constantly mindful of keeping it clean. Whenever you've paused and put down the airbrush – to make a pot of tea, answer the phone or even mix up a new colour – I'd advise you to at least spray a cupful of clean thinners through it first, before resuming spraying. This quick fix will help clear the head assembly of most of the paint residues and reduce the possibility of intractable deposits of pigment building up (they will accumulate anyway, but we can stave off their worst effects for as long as possible). The more thoroughly you go about this intermediate cleaning, the better the airbrush will perform when you resume work – a squirt of dirty thinners is not the same as a good sousing.

When you start spraying paint again, remember that the airbrush will still be full of thinners so you'll need to spray away to waste the ultra-watery stuff that comes out of the nozzle before pointing it at your model. But when I'm mixing weathering colours from the same palette, I don't need to purge all traces of the previous tone as thoroughly as I would if I were spraying livery colours and moving from, say, yellow to blue or red to white. Some blending effect may indeed be desirable in certain circumstances, but what we're really concerned with is achieving good paint-flow through the airbrush and onto the model.

When spraying continuously, say for 20 minutes of more, I'll often give the airbrush an interim clean anyway, just to slow down the rate of internal paint build-up. With experience, you start to sense the airbrush straining and the paint not coming through as smoothly as you'd like. At the same time, you may find the paint has started to thicken in the colour cup as the solvent evaporates, but a drop or two of thinners and a good stir should cure this. Again, it's best to test first before applying paint to the model.

When the job is done, I'll give the airbrush a particularly good cleaning with white spirit. I take the spray head off and, using kitchen roll and an old paintbrush, remove all visible traces of paint. I'll do the same with the needle and the colour cup and then reassemble it, blowing a cupful or two of neat thinners through it until it runs clear. It's tempting to hurry through this stage now that the excitement is over, but you'll only have to clean the airbrush properly next time you use it. (Being diligent, I do this anyway.)

Having cleaned out your airbrush after use, there's a lot there's a lot to be said for storing it in a disassembled state. If nothing else, it prevents odd bits of fluid collecting in areas with limited clearances, with the attendant risk they will dry out and cause blockages. Make sure, though, that the parts are not rattling around loose in an empty box. If you own more than one airbrush, keep them separate. When you want to use the airbrush again, reassemble it and away you go.

Unfortunately, enamel paint is tenacious stuff and acrylics are even more so as they dry so quickly. However careful you are with your cleaning routines, tiny deposits will start to build up in areas that elude the normal flushing-through routines with clean thinners. In my Iwata it's the paint tip; in the Badger 150 it's the needle bearing. After every five or six painting sessions, therefore, it's good practice to strip the airbrush down to its component parts and give it a thorough bath. If it's a new airbrush, have the instructions and especially the exploded view to hand, so you can be sure that everything goes back where it should. In the absence of the same, manufacturers' websites should be able to tell you what goes where.

First off is a preliminary soaking in cellulose thinners – an hour or so will help loosen hardened-off paint. Proprietary airbrush cleaners are available but I stick with cellulose thinners, which need to be treated with respect – I got some in my eyes once and their fumes are disgusting, so I always arrange adequate ventilation and protection. For best results, the airbrush needs to be completely dismantled before bathtime; most are broadly similar but some have more detachable pieces that come off, or come apart, and often have different names for the same component.

First I unscrew the paint regulator from the paint head and very carefully remove the paint tip. These are extremely delicate but, as they're usually made of brass, can be coaxed back to shape if there's any accidental distortion. Then I remove the head washer (if fitted) and clean it, not forgetting any deposits that have built up behind it. Finally I take out the needle and clean it thoroughly in cellulose thinners, before checking the tip under a powerful lens – if you can see it's slightly bent, smooth it out between your fingers and rub it with a circular motion on some super-fine emery to restore its shape.

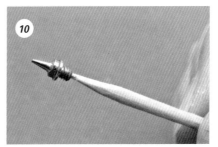

The needle tube can be unscrewed now and checked for paint (airbrushes can leak into unexpected places, usually the result of worn or missing seals and bearings); ditto the inside of the barrel and the needle bearing. On my elderly Badger the air valve sometimes gets sticky and, on inspection, shows traces of paint around the spring, so this may need careful dismantling and purging. On a newish airbrush, especially one of the better ones, this should not be necessary.

However thorough I try to be with my before-and-after cleaning routines, I'm astonished at how much gunk comes out of the business end of my airbrushes when they're fully stripped down and doused in thinners. These things are designed to work with fine water-soluble inks, remember, not heavy enamels or acrylics consisting of coarse particles of pigment. An hour's soak will soften all but the most stubborn build-up. Then I'll work away at each component in turn

10: One of the main places where pigment builds up is right inside the paint tip. If possible, remove the tip from the airbrush and very gently ream out the inside with a sharpened cocktail stick, liberally using cellulose thinners to dislodge stubborn deposits. The soft wood will absorb some of the paint but be very careful not to break the end off inside the paint tip – make a new reamer rather than risk this happening.

11: Keep going until as few traces as possible remain. It may be useful to thread some five-amp fuse wire through the paint tip, but take care not to damage anything. Put a bend in the wire so the paint tip cannot fall off.

12: When you replace the needle, you will probably find that a few drops of gunk (by now mostly made up of thinners) still ooze through. Wipe them off with your kitchen roll, taking care not to damage the delicate point of the needle. If you can't remove the paint tip, the next best way to clean it is by repeatedly pulling back the trigger to withdraw the needle, dipping the head in cellulose thinner and releasing the needle so that little drops of deconstructed paint build-up are forced one by one through the head assembly. It takes time to get rid of accumulated paint deposits this way but it can be done.

with wooden cocktail sticks and fine soft wire (five-amp fuse wire is very useful for cleaning inside paint tips), all the time washing and wiping the crud off and trying not to put more back in than I take out. Magnifying aids and an unforgiving eye will show you how areas you thought were scrupulously clean are anything but.

When satisfied all is as it should be, reassembly is the same as disassembly in reverse. Once you've dropped a tiny paint tip or needle bearing on the floor and spent an hour looking for it, you will learn to do it in good light on a sheet of white paper with your sleeves rolled up, so that they don't accidentally brush anything away. Blow more clean thinners through the airbrush; while it may take a few seconds to clear and for the working parts to reacquaint themselves with one another, you should now have a brush as fit for purpose as the day that you bought it.

Using weathering powders

Right: I'd airbrush-weathered this Bachmann 'G2a' 0-8-0 as a demonstration piece, but even when it had been coaled up and made ready for service I felt it was lacking something – the weathering was generic and had little localised detail. Weathering powders helped bring it to life.

Below left: I dabbed tiny quantities of MIG Light Rust (which has an orange tone) onto areas that would be regularly abraded, such as the coal rails and the inside of the bunker. Then I flicked most of it away with a soft brush before adding darker tints to the rear corners of the tender top.

Below: A little more fresh rust helps to build up the detailed effect. With these orange colours you have to be very sparing in your application, otherwise the effect looks badly overdone.

Far left: Now for some darker rust tones on the cab roof and firebox, to suggest more advanced corrosion. Rust darkens appreciably with age and exposure to the elements – the colour of old rust has a lot of purple in it. Flicking with a soft brush creates the effect of downward streaking.

Left: These soft foam wedges – from the cosmetics counter at Boots – are great for gently merging the colours built up by successive applications of powder.

Above left: More texturing of the powdered rust, this time via a small, stiffish makeup brush and flicking excess pigment away with a vertical motion.

Above: Adding a touch of MIG Track Brown to the tender sideframes, once again using a small make-up brush. This helps modulate the oily black of the axleboxes with the brake-block dust on the sideframes.

Left: The colours – whether airbrushed or powders – are all integrated with one another and nothing sings out aggressively.

Right: Tiny quantities of dark rust around the smokebox and chimney help bring the model to life.

Far right: I dusted a very fine coating of MIG Black Smoke over the boiler and streaked it using an old paintbrush dipped in airbrush cleaner.

Right: It's hard to tell where the airbrushing ends and the weathering powders begin. The subtle integration of elements is all important in achieving a convincing effect. Finding methods and materials that work for you is far more important than toeing the party line.

CHAPTER

6

Some Worked Examples

Spit and polish

Achieving an 'oily rag' finish on Great Northern

Roy Jackson wrested *Great Northern* out of a less than stellar Crownline kit. After being lined by Geoff Kent, it came to me with the brief that it should look 'pretty clean'. I was glad of the opportunity – as an 11-year-old spotter/tyro photographer, *Great Northern* was one of a few rarities that I saw but failed to record on film. I can remember it well enough, standing outside York shed looking very careworn. I even framed it in my Brownie viewfinder, but failed to press the shutter out of fear of what my father would say about a photograph clearly taken while trespassing on BR property. Half a century later, adding the finishing touches to this EM model somehow seemed to square the circle.

I also wanted to show how sympathetic weathering can improve the appearance of any model and help bring it into line with those of far higher overall quality. My interpretation was to present a locomotive that, having been in traffic for some considerable while since its last shopping, was actually quite dirty apart from those parts – boiler, cab and tender side sheets – that had been selectively cleaned for the sake of appearance. We like to think that at one time all express engines shone like the sun, but it's not true – some did, admittedly, but others were given only a perfunctory and superficial wipe-over, a quick trip through the carwash as opposed to a comprehensive valeting.

1: Great Northern *was an awkward-looking beast and its ill-proportioned lines cannot be improved by my weathering treatment. What I can do is to bestow a bit more credibility on its appearance by conveying the impression of a well-used locomotive that has been regularly cleaned. As we will see in a later section, this is a very different concept to an ex-works engine fresh from the paintshop. As it stands, the lone 'A1/1' looks like neither.*

3: The next stage is to tone down the shiny black of the running plate, which is another modelling convention not found in prototype practice. I'm using the same paint mix as before but with a hint more Matt Leather in it. The mask – which is simply a sheet of thin card – helps minimise the overspray landing on the boiler. We want to allow some hint of discoloration to creep onto the green, as this will form the basis of weathering effects that will be created in due course.

1

2: The first step is to begin work on eradicating the shiny black wheels and underpinnings only found on model railways. I've sprayed over them with a 70:30 mix of Humbrol Metalcote Gunmetal and Matt Leather. Of course, as soon as you've treated one area, the shortcomings of others immediately become apparent – in this case, the immaculate semi-matt paintwork of the boiler and cab, seldom if ever seen on a real locomotive. (More of this later.)

2

3

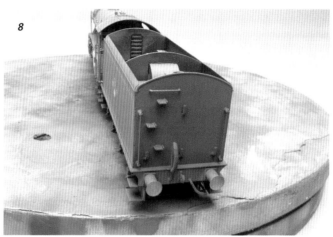

5: A touch more Metalcote Gunmetal can be added to the cab roof, which is invariably covered in soot and ash and never cleaned. Study of prototype pictures confirms that the optimum colour is a warm charcoal with a hint of brown – easily mixed from our basic two-colour weathering palette.

6: The smokebox is sprayed with the same colour mix, but with a few more drops of Gunmetal. Here's a clear illustration of the way paint looks different when wet – compare this with the next shot, which shows the same thing a few seconds later looking considerably lighter. Modern fast-drying paints make decision-making a lot easier and using an airbrush helps accelerate the process.

7: We can then go on to apply a similar light misting to the smokebox front, the running plate and the smoke deflectors. All that matt paint doesn't look terribly convincing, but that's because it needs further work before it's had time to harden off. The finish on the running plate is still a bit too regular and so some localised treatment is called for.

8 : Observation of the prototype confirms that the back of the tender is not always cleaned. In some cases it's as filthy as any freight locomotive and yet the tender sides, cab and boiler can be highly polished. Always copy what you see on the prototype rather than adopting a generic style of weathering.

4: You need to move around the whole locomotive in the manner shown – or at least all the black parts, such as the tender frames and the lower firebox area. We don't want saturation coverage, however, merely a toning down of the satin black in which they were painted. A little gentle unevenness is all to the good and I'd suggest adding an extra quantity of Leather at some stages just for variety.

9: The working parts of a locomotive include the cab area as well as the wheels and motionwork. The cab entrance and doors – if fitted – quickly show signs of human activity and the paint is invariably blackened, polished or worn as a result of enginemen in greasy overalls repeatedly climbing in and out. We can replicate this with a gentle mist of weathering on and around the handrails.

10: Here I'm spraying more of our sooty-brown mix onto the washout plugs, trying to build up the grubby deposits that accumulate in inaccessible places. If you don't have a quality airbrush it's probably best to add these little touches by hand – budget airbrushes give you very little control over paint delivery and direction.

11: A general dinginess is starting to build up around the non-liveried areas such as the cab steps, the Cartazzi truck, the wheels, the footplate, and so on. It's not terribly realistic at this stage, mainly because everything looks so flat and lifeless – we need to achieve more of a contrast between different surfaces, not a uniform matt finish.

12: Now I'm going to diffuse these sooty deposits on the green-liveried areas – including those that landed on the boiler while I was weathering the running plate – by brushing them away with a broad brush well moistened with thinners. It's best to work downwards from top to bottom.

13: I don't want to entirely eradicate the effects of discoloration, rather to encourage them to show up among the relief detail of the boiler, firebox and tender. In other words, we're replicating the effect of cleaning the locomotive with an oily rag. The shiny bit comes later.

16: I'm using a clapped-out No 2 brush to clean the tender bufferbeam. As well as taking much of the paint off, the thinners will flow in and leave a fine deposit that emphasises the relief.

17: This is the moment that always produces a gasp at my weathering tutorials. I dip my big, flat brush into a bottle of Johnson's Klear floor polish and start to brush it onto the parts of the model that I want to display a gleaming, 'oily rag' finish.

18: I apply the floor polish quite thickly – it seems to be self-levelling and tends not to leave brush marks, but I'm always careful to work vertically in either a downward or upward direction as appropriate. A measure of unevenness in the application may be no bad thing.

19: The polish looks quite horrible while wet, but I'm used to it by now and I can predict the results. The one thing you need to avoid is any blobby build-ups. Sometimes you get frothy bubbles forming, but this seems to sort itself out during the rapid drying process.

14: The green is no longer solid. There are subtle hints of blackening and other discoloration, though nothing like as intense as the weathering I've applied to the areas below the running plate. On the real thing, these would have been allowed to accumulate without attention from the cleaners, whereas the upper works will have been regularly wiped down.

15: The overspray on the tender has been washed with thinners and, while the finish is still an unconvincing semi-matt green, it now looks far less uniform in tone. You can see how brushing it away with a vertical motion creates a subtle variation of tone that prevents it looking like a solid green box. This will also help to suggest the rippling you find in panelwork – an area the size of a tender sidesheet or a diesel locomotive bodyshell is anything but flat.

20: After only five minutes' drying time, this is what we end up with from the first coat of Klear. The colours are deeper, richer and far more realistic than the unconvincing semi-matt Brunswick green we had before. The subtle streaking in the oily-rag effect is immediately apparent, contrasting with flat areas such as the cab roof, motionwork and tender top.

21: Once the polish is touch-dry, I can add a thin second coat just to beef up the finish. (You do not achieve anything by adding a third.) The firebox sides and front boiler ring appear to have been polished over the underlying dirt, exactly as on my reference photographs. The engine has been regularly cleaned but not too conscientiously, so over time patches of paint have become permanently discoloured.

22: I haven't put floor polish on the smokebox, as this are a very hot area and any shine rapidly burns off. Instead, I've gently rubbed the paintwork with a cotton bud to bring out the sheen of the Metalcote Gunmetal. Applied over satin-black paint it gives a wonderfully metallic look, but you need to allow time for it to dry.

23: As well as weathering being clearly visible under the gloss, I want to show what has happened since the engine was last cleaned – in other words, to add weathering over the coat of floor polish. The main constituent is a streak of soot – a thin mist of virtually neat Matt Black streamed on from the smokebox end, coating the top of the boiler. This effect is commonplace on the prototype. You can see from this angle how I've scuffed up the paint on the running plate by stabbing at it with a brush moistened by thinners.

24: The sheen of the oily-rag finish is looking good but the remaining work that needs to be done is apparent – the wheels look a bit flat (and need to be turned a half-revolution to allow us to get at the shadow behind the motionwork) and the valve gear has not been touched since we started work on the model. If nothing else, it shows how weathering is built up sequentially and doesn't all happen at once. The paintwork has been brought up to a very high level of finish and yet some parts are exactly as they were.

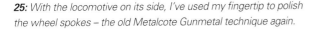

25: With the locomotive on its side, I've used my fingertip to polish the wheel spokes – the old Metalcote Gunmetal technique again.

26: With the driving wheels now looking suitably oily, I've at last turned my attention to the motionwork. Humbrol Tan No 9 is a very good colour for valve gear, but here I've decided to build up the effect by applying several colours sequentially, beginning with a glossy maroon.

27: After the initial maroon, I overpainted the motionwork with a variety of colours, including bauxite and tan, sometimes mixing them together to give colour variation.

28: The slight unevenness of finish given by the floor polish replicates the effect of the cleaners' rags and gives some interesting reflections. By request, I've left the buffer heads in their natural state to suggest an engine that's been rostered for a special working – a 'Northern Rubber Special', perhaps, or an Ian Allan Locospotter's Club excursion.

29: Great Northern *may have been a gauche-looking thing but models of it certainly attract attention. Green is unusual as a livery colour in that it darkens with age and exposure to the elements. On an otherwise clean engine, the hints of dinginess around the cab doors and along the top of the locomotive really help bring it to life.*

The big build-up

Creating the effect of accumulated grime on a Bachmann O4 2-8-0

I have a special regard for heavy freight locomotives, from 'WDs' and '9Fs' right the way through to American super-muscle such as 'Big Boys' and 'Alleghenies'. All feature strongly in my model locomotive collection and in my preferences for weathering projects.

There's an honesty about these bruisers that ties in with my affection for the everyday working railway. The intrinsic functionality of freight power usually results in a handsome design that stands the test of time; passenger locomotives, on the other hand, are more decorative in their styling and therefore more transient in their appeal.

Part of the attraction of heavy freight-haulers stems, I'm sure, from the heroic filthiness they generally exhibit. Outward cleanliness has no purpose in freight operations, so it can be dispensed with – the external appearance of a passenger design, on the other hand, has always been an important element in winning custom from fickle travellers.

In this regard, J. G. Robinson's 2-8-0s have long been a favourite. At sheds such as Langwith, Colwick and Doncaster, I used to revel in their degenerate appearance – all encrusted grime and severe lime-streaking. Numbers were frequently almost invisible; I'm sure I must have seen a clean 'Tiny', but I don't remember it.

Left: O4/8 No 63858 was a Doncaster regular for many years. The partial cleaning in this late-1950s view emphasises the contrast between solid black and the wonderfully variegated tones on the boiler, splasher and running plate. Notice the warmth in the colours – the steam locomotive was a highly animated piece of machinery. ©Colour-Rail.

Right: O4/8 No 63606 in standard condition for the class – and indeed for all Eastern Region heavy freight power. There is limescaling everywhere (the East Midlands had notoriously hard water), the nether regions are liberally coated in brake dust and the paint has flaked badly on the tender coping. These engines did a fair amount of shunting and the out-of-kilter buffer beam is evidence of a clumsy hand at the regulator. T B Owen ©Colour-Rail.

1: As far as the external finish is concerned, it's impossible to recall a 'Tiny' looking like the out-of-the-box Bachmann model. Even ex-works, they looked like they'd been painted with cheap household gloss applied with a distemper brush. Everything else about this model is superb, however – one of the most accurate RTR steam locomotives ever released. This was the first Bachmann 'O4' to run on Retford, instantly shaming the hordes of K's 2-8-0s that had held sway since High Dyke days and earlier.

2: I mixed up a brownish concoction of Humbrol Matt Leather and Matt Black and began spraying it freehand onto the frames and running gear. There was no need to be concerned about paint drifting over the cab and tender sides, as it all adds to the general effect of a very grubby locomotive. Notice how close in I'm spraying, using a lot of air to ensure adequate atomisation of the paint while being sparing with the delivery of paint.

3: We can progress around the whole locomotive in this way, gently building up a brownish track colour over the wheels and frames. Here I'm extending the colour onto the buffer beams and front platform. At this stage of the process we are simply putting on a generic base coat, over which several subsequent applications of more detailed weathering will be misted. The final appearance will only begin to take shape much later on.

4: It's easy to miss areas such as the tops of the frames under the running plate, the portion of the wheel spokes obscured by the motionwork or the underside of the buffers. To get at these areas you may need to tip the locomotive on its side – this is best done now, to avoid scuffing up freshly applied weathering on the upper works.

5: This is what we end up with after the initial round with the airbrush – it's only taken a couple of minutes, if that, to get this far. The locomotive looks just like a 'factory-weathered' model, because the simple dusting-up process I've just described is all you get from the RTR people. But what we have here is only the very beginning not a final statement.

6: The next stage is to make up a quantity of the weathering mix with a lot more black in it, so that it comes out as a warm sooty grey. I've sprayed this lightly over the body, not allowing it to build up to any degree and making sure I get it into awkward areas such as the corner where the cab front meets the firebox. I'm sure many people would settle for this as it stands, but to my eye it entirely lacks the subtle variety of tone that makes for truly realistic weathering. This can only come from repeated tonal applications and delicate hand-finishing.

7: Now I'm starting to overpaint the upper works with a deeper brown mix, using at least double the quantity of Matt Leather. I'm spraying on a gentle mist and applying it in large, drifting, irregular patches devoid of any clear outline. The orange-brown gunk that coated many steam locomotives was not rust but brake-block dust that built up in a thick film, totally obscuring the livery beneath. As it did not interfere with the working of the locomotive, it was left undisturbed.

8: You can see how I'm starting to work up a variety of tones on the boiler – a black locomotive can look like a silhouette moving around your layout, unless you take the trouble to break down that solid outline. Note that the coverage is intentionally uneven, but not wildly so. The variation of colour should be obvious but, at the same time, as subtle as you can possibly make it. Red rust and sooty black do not look good together, whereas a few variations on the theme of a warm, brownish grey will work wonders. It doesn't take too much time or effort to get to this stage – if this was how factory-weathered RTR locomotives looked then I'd find them a lot more acceptable.

9: Freight locomotives – even the big ones like this 2-8-0 – did a fair amount of tender-first running and not just on light-engine moves. I like to see this replicated on a layout and make a particular effort with the tender rear, building up little gradations of colour while staying within the one overall theme. The red of the buffer beam would be almost totally obscured and, in many cases, indistinguishable from the rest of the locomotive.

10: The area to the rear of the bunker is always unkempt, even on an express locomotive. There's usually a fair bit of water slopping around which, mixed with highly acidic coal dust, results in corrosion. This is represented not by a glaring red but by an altogether subtler shade of orange, as if we were looking at the locomotive from a good hundred feet away. Colours tone down remarkably when seen over that kind of distance.

11: Now I'm adding a darker tint to the motionwork, to suggest the oily patina of working metal that, in many cases, spills over on to the brake hangers. This view gives a good impression of the different shades that can be built up from just two colours. Note again the ever-shifting variation of hue, without clear outline but within strict tonal limits. Getting thus far has taken exactly 15 minutes of concentrated effort.

12: After the initial application of paint, I find it worthwhile to put down the airbrush and take stock. If you blaze ahead regardless, you tend to end up with a severely over-egged pudding. Paint-pause-think-paint-pause-think works very well as a methodology (especially if you're a tea drinker, like me). After half an hour or so, your head clears and the way forward suddenly seems a lot more obvious.

13: Retrospection enabled me to see how the 'Tiny' looked a bit cold at this stage – it lacked the spark of animation that comes from a hint of warmer colours. This is not a matter of simply painting the locomotive brown – it's more a case of adding warm highlights in areas that would justify them. First off was the smokebox, always one of the hottest parts of a locomotive, where the paint often burns away and exposes the metal beneath, leading to corrosion.

14: Tender rears get splashed with road dirt thrown up by the wheels. There's also a tendency to rust wherever you have large quantities of water in contact with metal. Airbrushing a hint of rusty discoloration around the bottom of the tender rear is the kind of detail that suggests a gradual build-up of layers of grime from a variety of sources.

15: The same reddish mix – achieved simply by increasing the proportion of Matt Leather – can be applied to the brakes and the surrounding area of the tender frames. Nothing too stark and contrasting, or which would be clearly visible a hundred yards away, is required – just something a touch brighter and redder. Suggestion is infinitely preferable to overstatement.

16: *Airbrushing more rusty discoloration, this time on the inside of the bunker. I've already put some on the inside corners of the rear coping. High-level views of tender tops are hard to find – a pure black tender interior would be wildly improbable, even on a freshly shopped locomotive, and yet this is how you so often see them on layouts.*

17: *I can really feel the locomotive coming to life now, as the greys and browns begin to work together to create a deliciously varied overall coating. This is the kind of condition in which most heavy freight engines spent much of their lives, even in pre-nationalisation days. To present them otherwise – especially if you have a large fleet of them, as we do at Retford – is to risk distorting reality.*

18: *Time now for an altogether darker and greyer mix to represent the soot and ash that beats down from the chimney, liberally coating the top of the boiler and firebox, the boiler fittings and the cab roof. Coal smoke is filthy stuff and it should be apparent. A thick black line is not required, just an intensification of the effect over the affected areas.*

19: *Notice the general darkening along the top of the boiler and firebox and the way in which I've taken the shine off the dome. This kind of weathering is all about cumulatively adding realism to your models one stage at a time. Once again you can see how wet paint is a very different colour to how it appears when it dries. You can gradually learn to predict the effects and to allow for them – but until then you have to take this transformation on faith.*

20: *Reaching the end of the second phase of weathering took another quarter of an hour. The effects are starting to look pretty well integrated and no one part of the locomotive stands out as radically different to any other. Everything you see here has been created using the airbrush freehand, but now we can start to think about adding some more specific weathering effects to give this particular locomotive a subtly distinctive appearance.*

21: *From this angle, the soot along the top half of the boiler works really well with the almost orange shade of the smokebox. One-tone overall weathering looks very unnatural, but so does an approach that uses a multitude of different paint colours. The shifts in tone need to be small but significant – if you can achieve this, then your weathering will really bring your models to life.*

22: *Bachmann's highly detailed cab interior is typical of modern RTR offerings. I appreciate this, as I've always enjoyed adding an equally meticulous plethora of pipes, handwheels, gauges and valves to my hand-built models. The gleaming copper pipework is a bit questionable on a freight locomotive, but the warm, dark grey knocks it back to more acceptable levels while ensuring the detail remains visible. The front coal plate on the tender can be treated in much the same way.*

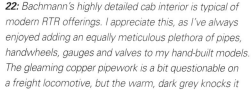

23: *An effect often seen on a steam locomotive – especially when operating in a hard-water area – is vertical streaking down the sides of the boiler. This is the result of priming in the cylinders which causes clouds of greasy water to be violently ejected out of the chimney. It lands on the top of the boiler and runs down its flanks, collecting on the lower half and bringing with it the soot and ash that's been ejected. If there is limescale present, over time it can build up into substantial deposits. My method of recreating the effects of priming begins by scalpelling a couple of slits into a header card.*

24: *This card is then trimmed to form a mask that will slip in behind the boiler handrail, avoiding the stanchions. Shaped into a gentle curve it acts as a stencil, allowing you to airbrush over the top to create little streaks of weathering on the boiler. To avoid drift, you need to spray from pretty close in but with a lot less paint than you might imagine. The key thing is to keep everything vertical, so it helps to use a header card that contains parallel lines that can be used as an alignment aid.*

25: *To represent the effects of priming I mix up a pale-greyish beige from Matt White, Matt Black and Matt Leather, gradually moving along the boiler, spraying one small section at a time and avoiding regular patterns of streaking. Here again we have an effect that, at its best, is built up gradually over repeated applications – although I'd add the caveat that, while it's not particularly time-consuming, it does call for intense concentration. As with many aspects of weathering, understatement is everything.*

26: *After the first pass with the airbrush, I've added a spot more Matt Leather to the beige limescaling and sprayed on a few more streaks, using the same mask. The difference in colours is not great but it will still be noticeable. The reversing rod and blower pipe have acquired zebra stripes – this is inevitable (unless you go in for some hideously complicated masking) but, as such tiny quantities of paint are involved, the problem can be easily remedied.*

27: *Add streaks to the other side at the same time, using the same colours. I vary the application from a gentle waft to a good blast from close in – using slits of different widths, you can create anything from a delicate pencil stroke to a hard line. There will be inevitably an element of randomness but this is all to the good. I've managed to get some slight overspray on the top half of the boiler – but this is neither here nor there, as we will see.*

28: *Making a third pass, with some greyer streaks here and there – all told, it took me just 20 minutes. You can go on to add more layers, but the returns diminish and pretty soon it starts to look a bit forced and the colours become increasingly indistinct. At this stage they are a little raw still, but this will be toned down with a touch of general toning-down so that the limescaling no longer looks like it's superimposed on top of the weathering.*

29: *This is how we get rid of the overspray – by making another mask and spraying a sooty grey-black along the top of the boiler, blending it in with the existing weathering that represents soot and ash deposits. Only a couple of passes will be needed to 'vanish' the offending streaks of limescaling. For reasons that will become clear, I've used Metalcote Gunmetal as well as Matt Black in this particular mix.*

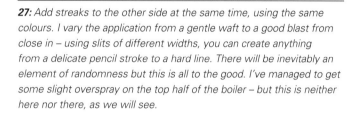

30: *The final stage is to airbrush a gentle mist of brownish-grey weathering over the limescaling. This will tone it down and integrate it with the weathering as a whole, suggesting the accumulation of archaeological layers of filth. Knocking the limescaling back like this also helps create the muted effect of colours seen from a distance.*

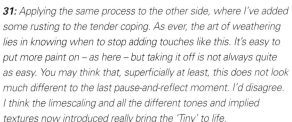

31: *Applying the same process to the other side, where I've added some rusting to the tender coping. As ever, the art of weathering lies in knowing when to stop adding touches like this. It's easy to put more paint on – as here – but taking it off is not always quite as easy. You may think that, superficially at least, this does not look much different to the last pause-and-reflect moment. I'd disagree. I think the limescaling and all the different tones and implied textures now introduced really bring the 'Tiny' to life.*

32: *Now I'm going to take a large, barely damp brush and gently draw it down the top half of the boiler, to suggest the effect of rainwater causing the ash and soot deposits to break down into streaks. This is another of those subliminal effects that are hardly noticeable. When the paint has hardened off, I'll flick at the streaks with a clean, dry brush to bring out the sparkle in the Metalcote Gunmetal. Just under two hours have passed – including thinking time – since I started work on this locomotive. I'm now going to set the work aside for 24 hours to allow the paint to harden and give me time to consider what I want to do next.*

33: *As well as smoke, steam and ash, all kinds of muck gets thrown out of the chimneys of hard-working locomotives – especially those running on poor coal and bad water – and you get some splendid dribbles running down the smokeboxes of engines from hard-water areas. Working from a photograph, I stippled on paint using a wooden cocktail stick, flicking it into streaks with a fine sable brush.*

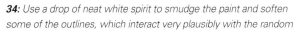

34: *Use a drop of neat white spirit to smudge the paint and soften some of the outlines, which interact very plausibly with the random marks created by dabbing on neat pigment with a stick. A gentle toning down with the airbrush will blend everything in nicely. The streaking of soot and ash deposits on the boiler is readily apparent from this angle, where the Gunmetal catches the light.*

35: *My treatment of 63607 was based very closely on two photographs of shabby-looking O4s, one of them with a pronounced streak of rust-coloured slurry spilling out of a firebox washout plug. Using a wooden cocktail stick to give an irregular effect, I dabbed on some neat Matt Leather let down with a little Matt White. Once again, an overall waft with the airbrush will help everything bed in and give the impression of ancient encrustation. It's easy to overdo textured effects – in 4mm scale at least – but I think it works well here.*

36: *A bit of hand-stippled rust on one of the mudhole covers and airbrushed discoloration around the whistle, once again copied from a reference photograph.*

37: *You find all kinds of scars and dribbles on a smokebox front, indicative of the fierce chemical battle being fought within. Sometimes the heat is sufficient to burn the paint off the smokebox door and encourage corrosion.*

38: *We don't need anything too stark but we want our hand-applied effects to add something to the overall impression – hence the subtle toning-down and blending-in here. Note how many colours there are in the buffer beam – except red. The buffer heads show similar variety and yet everything is in the same part of the spectrum.*

39: *Welds, seams and lines of rivets often show signs of distress in later life and leaking tender tanks are an inevitable consequence. On the real thing it's a common weathering effect, but it's also far from universal and it needs to be applied with some restraint. Having already airbrushed some rusty discoloration along the tender coping, I've hand-painted some clear signs of leakage on the lower part of the tender body, using a Matt Leather/Matt White mix. Gravity ensures water flows down to earth, but as it follows the line of least resistance, avoiding obstacles in its path, its course may not be truly vertical. In weathering, a measure of considered randomness is always A Good Thing.*

40: *I've dusted a thin, dark mist over the corrosion marks to knock them back into believability. Here, the suggestion is that this is a leak that was fixed months, if not years, ago. Further deposits of filth have built up in the meantime, creating a layered effect.*

41: *Working parts such as the motionwork and mechanical lubricators are usually swimming in oil. There are several ways of representing this, the easiest of which is to paint the parts with gloss varnish. In my reference photographs the spokes of the pony wheels are oily too, so they can be treated at the same time.*

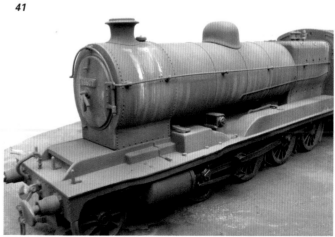

42: Handrails and grab irons often show signs of inadvertent polishing, easily replicated by painting them with Metalcote Gunmetal, applied with a fine brush. I've already polished the tender brake handle and now I'm using a cotton bud on the cab handrails.

43: The end result: I spent a good two hours adding the hand-finished effects, on top of a similar amount of time the previous day spent creating the basic weathering. With nothing else to do – except add a healthy load of crushed coal in the tender – I put away my paints and brushes.

44: The left-hand side of the 'Tiny' is clearly of a piece with its opposite, but, as on a real locomotive, there are many points of difference. The rusting around the tender coping shows up well here, as does the streaking and fading on the boiler.

Right: The contrast with the out-of-the-box model is profound, completely altering its character as well as its plausibility in a layout context.

Not as clean as you'd think

Replicating MacCailin Mor *not long out of works*

Most trains on model railways – passenger and freight – are worked by ex-works locomotives. They're not just clean, they look as if they're straight out of the paint shop (represented in our case by the tight-fitting cardboard packaging from which they've just been prised, inevitably with some minor damage to detail).

On the real railway, ex-works locomotives are so rare that you always take a photograph of them. All the same, people still want to run them on their layouts, although a real ex-works locomotive looks nothing like we imagine it – still less like a brand-new model. Even if it's only run a couple of hundred miles since release from shops, it will show clear signs of use. There may not be the wholesale accumulation of dirt that you'd find on a hard-working engine, built up over time into a rich and varied patina, but it will be there all the same.

Apart from being a contradiction in terms (superficially at any rate), weathering an ex-works engine makes for an interesting project. It's quite a challenge to execute because it calls for exceptional levels of restraint if you're to retain that newly-shopped look, on what is clearly a working locomotive and not a museum piece. If you can create a convincing ex-works engine then, in my view, you can do almost anything.

1: Roy Jackson built this EM gauge model from a much-mauled PDK kit; Geoff Kent did the lining. The brief was for a recently ex-works engine that has completed a bit of running-in on the main line and is now ready to return to service. This explains the appearance of the solitary 'K1/1' Mogul – Eastfield's No. 61997, MacCailin Mor – on a light engine move through Retford. We can assume that, like many engines on running-in turns from Doncaster, it's going down to Barkston on the GN main line where it will turn on the triangle and return, either to the plant for further attention or to 36A, to be made ready for the journey back to Scotland.

2: For a change I started at the top of the engine, spraying a light sooty coating over the smokebox and the top of the boiler. The paint was mixed from Metalcote Gunmetal with a proportion of Humbrol Matt Leather. I'm spraying with a lot of air from a couple of inches away and being careful not to let the paint build up – a thin waft is all we need.

3: I'm spraying the same weathering mix onto the wheels and motion, just to knock them back a little. An ex-works engine starts to get dirty the second it leaves the paint shop; once it's in steam, it will only be a matter of hours before soot, ash, oil and brake-block dust start to build up. (The idea that it would stay spotless for months is a myth perpetuated by modellers.) I'm seeking to recreate the appearance of an engine that's been out of shops for perhaps a week, mostly on running-in turns but with the possibility of being borrowed for a couple of days by an opportunist shedmaster.

4: Buffers do not shine – except on Royal Train engines and those rostered for enthusiasts' specials. Normally, they're the first thing to get dirty.

4

5: The top of the cab gets a good sooting as soon as the fire is lit. Throughout this preliminary weathering I'm using the same group of colours to ensure consistency. As ever, Humbrol Matt Leather, Revell Matt Black and Metalcote Gunmetal are the essential ingredients, mixed in various proportions according to need.

6: Now we come down to the running plate, which is always grubby even on an ex-works engine. I've gently misted over the buffers' shanks – the paint overspray here will be worked by hand at a later stage. The running plate will receive more detailed attention.

7: One of the first areas to get dirty is the cab entrance – crews climb in, shovelfuls of ash get thrown out and there's always plenty of coal dust about. Using very little pressure and even less paint, I'm adding a fine mist of discoloration around the cab doors and handrails. Again, this can be worked on later by hand if required, using a brush loaded with thinners to take some of it off. With enamels, there is plenty of time to build up subtle effects before the paint dries.

8: Rather than weather one side of the model and then the other, I'll do each bit separately, swinging it round on the painting turntable. I'll weather the wheels on one side, then the wheels on the other, cab steps on one side, cab steps on the other, and so on. As often as not, a change in paint mix is necessary anyway.

5

6

7

8

9

9: With the gentle weathering of the wheels, running plate and cab roof, you can see how the locomotive is starting to lose its box-fresh look. Yet the black paint remains glossy – as it will throughout, but only relative to the locomotive as a whole. The initial weathering-down is achieved with the same mix, mostly Metalcote Gunmetal with a proportion of Humbrol Matt Leather.

10: The tender top gets dirty very quickly, mostly on account of all that coal dust swirling around. The tender front can be similarly dusted down, but much of the dirt build-up evident around the buffers needs to be washed off with thinners.

10

11: The tender will be fully coaled later so we don't need to bother much about the bunker, but the rear tender platform would not stay shiny black for more than a few hours. After the first trip through the coaling plant it would be covered in coal dust and other detritus.

12: All that's initially needed is a bit of discoloration on the back of the tender to suggest a working engine, rather than a museum piece. The paint is a 60:40 mix of Revell Matt Black and Humbrol Matt Leather.

13: The tender frames get grubby quite quickly. One run from Doncaster to Barkston and return would be quite enough to knock back that paintshop gleam, especially if the weather were poor. I'm airbrushing on a light coat of grime with a bit more Leather in the mix.

14: The same warmer mix can go on the wheels and mainframes, suggesting a fine powdering of brake-block dust and road dirt. I'm not obscuring the weathering that's already in place – rather, I'm discreetly overpainting it to give a subtle variety of tones.

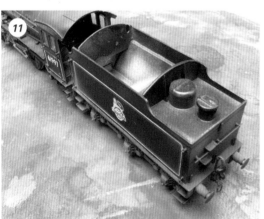

11

13

12

14

15

16

15: *My digital camera records that it's taken us exactly 17 minutes and two seconds to get this far. I'm pleased with the way things are looking. The impression of unusual cleanliness, offset by hints that this is, after all, a working locomotive, is exactly what I was aiming for. It has been achieved entirely by (a) powers of observation and (b) exercising restraint. Many modellers would be satisfied with things as they are, but I want to take them further. First, though, I'm going to put* MacCailin Mor *to one side for a few hours while I gather my thoughts.*

16: *After due deliberation and further study of my reference pictures, Ive decided to replicate the effect of a spot of priming thats sent dirty water shooting out of the chimney and over the boiler. The first step is to spray some neat Metalcote Gunmetal over the top of the boiler.*

17

17: *Now I've taken a half-inch flattie brush, moistened it with thinners and very gently wiped as much Gunmetal as I could off the boiler, stroking it in a downward motion to mimic the effect of water running down the barrel. This continued until it was almost all gone and just a hint remained, without touching the Gunmetal paint on the smokebox.*

18

18: *The streaking effect is barely perceptible and yet it makes a huge difference to the appearance of the boiler, which is no longer a solid black shape. The gleam of the metallic particles catches the light and suggests texture where there is none. I've buffed up the Gunmetal on the smokebox to enhance the shine. The weathering on the running plate, however, looks far too even and will receive attention in due course.*

19: *I did the same with the tender, mimicking the effect of rainwater washing coal dust down the sidesheets. This would be good interim state for a fairly clean engine, but I'm going to take quite a bit more off to get that not-quite-ex-works look. The paint will remain workable for a good couple of hours after application, so you can keep taking it off until you have the effect you want.*

19

20: While it's in the colour cup, I'm spraying neat Metalcote Gunmetal onto the tender axleboxes to suggest the oil that always collects in this area.

21: You can either leave the Gunmetal 'dry' on the axleboxes to suggest caked-on oil – which always acquires a flat appearance – or you can polish it with your fingertips or a cotton bud, yielding an altogether more oily look. All six axleboxes need not be the same; I've varied the treatment to add visual interest. This is the kind of detailed weathering that really brings a model to life.

22: Oil spillage around the mechanical lubricators helps build up the impression of a working locomotive. We don't want anything too extreme, just a bit of carelessness while the engine was being oiled round prior to release into traffic.

23: Footplates are always grubby – enginemen and disposal staff prefer it that way because there's less risk of slipping while clambering about, especially after dark. I've sprayed on a thin mist (60% Matt Leather, 40% Matt Black) and taken much of it off again by dabbing with a cotton bud moistened with white spirit, to suggest footmarks scuffing up the ash and road dust. Once again, breaking up the flat surface makes the model look a lot more three-dimensional.

24: The engine is still very clean and the only weathering is a light dusting such as an engine might pick up after a couple of hundred miles – there has been no time for heavy deposits of grime to build up. You will see a similar effect on a preserved steam locomotive after a mainline run – it may start off immaculate, but it always comes home grubby. That is the nature of the beast.

25

25 This is my idea of what an ex-works engine actually looks like, which is far from a clean locomotive. The main difference is that the weathering is quite superficial – it lacks the heavy accumulations of dirt and grime that build up on an engine in service and cannot be eradicated with an oily rag. All we need now is some coal in the tender and MacCailin Mor will be ready to head back to Scotland, assuming Doncaster district do not hang on to it for trip workings – much to the delight of the local spotters.

Fading fast

Using colour filters to create a sun-bleached look

Looking to create a faded, time-worn effect on an EWS-liveried Bachmann 08, I tried some new techniques and materials imported from the USA – a range of ultra high-quality weathering paints marketed by leading airbrush manufacturer Iwata under the Real Deal banner (see p.49). These acrylic colours are specially formulated for airbrushing but conventional brush-painting is perfectly feasible. The pigment is very fine, more akin to a filter, allowing you to build up incredibly subtle effects through multiple applications.

1: This 08 is in typical mid-noughties condition. The yellow has faded badly and the rest of the bodywork is almost as bad. I wanted to present a loco in a similar stage of degeneration, with oil-stained EWS maroon bleached almost pink in places.

2: The starting point for this experiment in techniques and materials was a Bachmann 08 in EWS livery. It's basically the out-of-the-box model with a few essential refinements such as fuel filler pipework, larger and more accurately positioned front-end air tanks, wire handrails and so on.

3: The translucent Iwata/Real Deal colours are applied as a thin mist over the existing paintwork, effectively acting as a filter that subtly modulates the underlying colour. Here I'm spraying on a very fine coating of the 'Light Dust' – a pinky beige colour, almost a skintone – over Bachmann's version of EWS maroon. The idea is to build up the effects of paint fade through successive applications. Although the method is akin to standard watercolour techniques of underpainting and overpainting, the consistency of the acrylic medium is exactly right for airbrushing and no dilution is required.

4: Now I've turned my attention to the rear of the cab and I'm starting to knock back the wasp stripes. I masked the windows to avoid overspray, but subsequently found you can wash the Iwata paints off with Vallejo airbrush cleaner without leaving any of the milky residue that most conventional thinners cause on clear glazing.

5: After two or three gentle applications of 'Light Dust' the EWS colours are starting to look distinctly faded, especially on the bonnet. Having cleaned out the airbrush I've begun adding some oily patches and general discoloration using a combination of 'Transparent Smoke' and 'Blue-gray Smoke'. I felt I'd rather overdone it on the middle equipment cabinet, so I took the paint off using more Vallejo airbrush cleaner and then made another application of 'Light Dust'.

6: Using darker tones to create false shadows around the edges of the roof panels enhances the three-dimensional effect. I use the airbrush for the initial application of weathering but its smoothly blended tones need roughing up with improvised hand tools. Here I'm taking paint off the cab roof using airbrush cleaner applied with an old sable brush, flicking it in a downward motion to simulate the effects of rainwater.

7: Now I'm using 'Soft Dirt' to represent the deposits that build up around an 08's nether regions. As a rule the outside frames stay pretty black and don't show the thick ochre-coloured coating that collects on the underframes of other classes. Using a high-quality airbrush allows me to

come in very close and deliver minimal quantities of colour.

8: I've just airbrushed some more 'Blue-gray Smoke' around the fuel tanks and misted an extra touch of fade over the cab roof. Note how the original livery colours still show through – nothing is obscured by heavy weathering. Using a blend of 'Light Dust' and 'Soft Dirt', the exhaust panel has been underpainted ready for treatment with weathering powders.

9: *High-level view – I've treated the exhaust area with 'Light Rust', 'Track Brown' and 'Dark Mud' and dusted tiny quantities of the latter two around the cab roof area. Only a minute amount is necessary – leave the overdone 'total decrepitude' approach to the military modellers.*

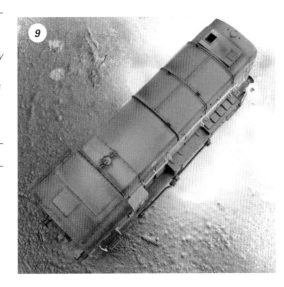

10: *MIG 'Gunmetal' weathering pigment gives a gentle lift to the fuel spillage on the tanks, the cab steps, the buffer shanks and the sideframes – when polished, the metallic particles embedded in the pigment give off a wonderfully convincing sheen. Contrary to popular belief, weathering effects are not always totally matt and a bit of shine here and there really brings a model to life. See also how oily dirt has built up in the crevices around the cab doors.*

11: *The transfer lettering on EWS locomotives seems to fade faster than the livery colours. A fibreglass burnishing brush is great for taking off the logo to create a prototypical 'distressed' look. Always work downwards to simulate the effect of rainwater gradually washing away the paint. I will go over this area again in due course with the 'Light Dust' filter to smooth over the raw edges exposed by the abrasive action of the brush.*

13: *The 08s – as I have known them for more than 50 years – are graceless, brutally functional locomotives that are most at home in an equally austere working environment. While some of the survivors are treated as pets, an outward air of neglect is infinitely more fitting.*

12: *You could just as well apply a well-diluted enamel or acrylic paint, but here I'm using a US-made product called 'Blackwash' (see p.52) to simulate the effects of dirt build-up in the radiator vanes, throwing them into sharper relief. It consists of a very fine purple-black pigment in a carrier solution which I imagine is isopropyl alcohol. The carrier evaporates, leaving the pigment that has collected by capillary action in the recessed areas. I use it to emphasise panel lines on plastic mouldings.*

Yorkshire coal-hauler

Trying some new techniques on a sector-livery Class 56

Although I've been weathering railway models since the early 1960s, my techniques continue to evolve. These days I could probably airbrush a convincing finish on a locomotive with my eyes closed, but there's always something new to try in my endless quest for realism.

Recently I've been experimenting with designers' gouache, a water-based product that you can buy in artists' supply shops. High-end American railroad modellers have used it for some time and I've been amazed at the results that can be obtained. Compared with good old Humbrols it gives fantastically subtle effects, but application takes time and patience. It's not unknown for the US pacesetters to spend months weathering a single model.

On this Class 56 I've combined gouache weathering on the bodysides with conventional airbrushing and powder pigment on the underframe and roof. The project therefore becomes a summary of everything that's gone before – but also an affirmation of my belief that we need to be constantly reassessing our work and looking at new techniques and technologies.

1: The starting point is Hornby's Class 56, seen here in late-production guise as 56128 West Burton Power Station. It's a good-enough model but amenable to a little refinement in terms of detail – especially the grillework.

2: Having stripped it of its West Burton Power Station *identity with a fibreglass brush, I improved the base Hornby model with a host of aftermarket detail parts from Brian Hanson's Extreme Etchings range. The new side and roof grilles make a huge difference – to prevent the fine detail clogging up, however, they need only the faintest mist of primer. Rather than the coarse acrylic stuff you get from car accessory shops, I prefer Teroson etch primer from the Loctite range. Odd gaps are filled with Squadron green putty.*

3: Because of the different weathering treatments planned for this model, I carried out most of the work with the body separated from the chassis. I weathered the latter using a Badger 150 airbrush, beginning with a light all-round coat of underframe gunk, concocted inevitably from Humbrol Matt Leather and Matt Black.

4: Here I'm putting on a lighter coat of the same mix, applied to the springing units and other areas that, in my reference photographs, are clearly a different shade. Getting the airbrush low-down and parallel to the painting turntable ensures even paint coverage – the temptation is always to spray from on high, which does not work. To do this you need to take off the clunky colour cup.

5

5: Now for something a little darker, once again copying what I've seen in photographs. Notice how the weathering is already starting to bring out the detail in the underframe mouldings – you see very little of this when they're solid black.

6

6: Time for a few wafts of almost-neat track colour. The Badger airbrush lacks the ultra-fine control of my Iwata, so I'll need to work on these areas to blend them in a bit more subtly with a spot of Metalcote Gunmetal.

7

7: The object of using the Badger for this particular project was to show how you can overcome the limitations of a less refined airbrush. Because of the comparative lack of precision, I'm aiming it below the workpiece and just catching the brake-operating levers and springing units with the overspray.

8

9

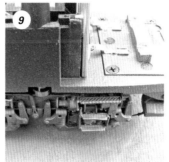

8: Bogie steps are always heavily polished by the crewmen's boots and the best way to represent this is with Gunmetal pigment from the MIG range. At this stage I've only applied it to the bottom step. You only need a tiny amount on the tip of a small paintbrush, size 0 or 1. Dab it on and then flick away at it to achieve the polished effect.

9: Now I've done all three steps and the transformation is remarkable, especially the chequerplate on the top step. A model really comes to life through these subtle contrasts between matt and shiny, light and dark, clean and grubby.

10

10: Having gently polished the Metalcote Gunmetal applied to the brake-operating levers, I added a touch more MIG weathering powder – Dark Mud this time – using a small makeup brush as an applicator. Once again, the effects appear random but are faithfully copied from reference photographs.

11

11: A not uncommon feature of Class 56s – and of Class 86 AC electrics, for that matter – was a replacement compressor unit still in primer. In my reference photographs 56075 featured this on one side, and so my model does too. I mixed up some very thin beige-grey from Humbrols and flooded it on with a No 2 brush. To avoid brushstrokes use the biggest paintbrush and the thinnest paint you can get away with.

12: Before starting on the roof, I masked of the sides and cab ends using Betto tape – a paper-based product used by aeromodellers. I made a series of passes with subtly varied colour mixes.

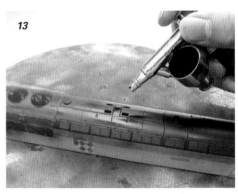

13: The area around the exhaust outlets is always a pure, sooty black – and is also the first part of a roof to get dirty. A diesel will not need to run many miles before this part of the roof is well blackened.

14: The dark grey in the triple-grey Railfreight livery is a good match for a well-weathered roof, which I assume is why it was chosen. It's quite difficult in this kind of light to see any difference, but I can assure you that it's there.

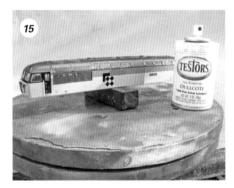

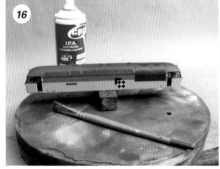

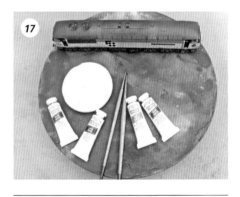

15: The next stage is to spray the body with Testor's Dullcote – the best solid-matt finish I've ever used. When dry (allow a full 24 hours if you possibly can) it forms a solid key onto which some very subtle effects can be worked.

16: I sprayed some isopropyl alcohol into a saucer and then, using a half-inch flattie brush, worked vertically, painting the bodysides with it in parallel streaks. This subtly fades the grey paintwork, which is a touch on the dark side on the out-of-the-box Hornby model.

17: Weathering bodywork with gouache is totally different to any other method I've tried. I apply it to my models as an artist would apply it to a canvas – paint brush in one hand, piece of rag in the other, chosen colours ready to be squeezed out into the palette. Once it's mixed, I'll pick up the colour on my brush, dip it in dilute isopropyl alcohol – which helps break up surface tension – and apply it with vertical strokes, touching up accordingly and applying less or more pigment as required in particular areas.

18: Having looked closely at my reference pictures (pp38-39), the first step is to dab on a little Raw Sienna along the lower bodyside edges, to mimic the effect of road dirt thrown up from the track. The paint is applied neat with a round-tipped No 3 brush.

19: *Once it's dry – which takes only a few minutes – I can start to remove or thin the gouache with water in areas where I feel heavy colour application is unnecessary, as with the cab sidesheet here. This is all part of the process – putting paint on and taking it off again to obtain the effect you require.*

20: *Cotton buds moistened with water are useful for creating streaks or just gently moving pigment around. Adding a few drops of car windscreen wash gives you control over how much gouache is removed – the higher the proportion of screenwash, the more gouache comes off. A 50/50 mix is the default setting.*

21: *When I'm satisfied, I can spray that area of the model with more Testor's Dullcote. This will permanently seal the colour in place and allow me to build up fresh effects over the top without affecting what's beneath. Until the gouache has been fixed with Dullcote, I can work it as much as I like – I can even take it off completely if I'm not happy with the results. No other weathering medium has this flexibility.*

22: *For this next phase I've switched from Raw Sienna to Burnt Umber, dabbing it around the bodyside panels where dirt would build up. The effects are built up through repeated applications, preferably starting with the lightest colour, alternately adding and removing paint.*

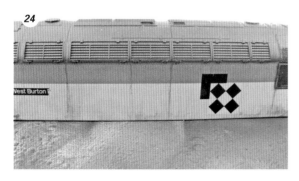

23: *We've made three or four applications here: paint the gouache on; wipe some or most of it off; spray with Dullcote; paint some more gouache on, in a slightly different colour this time; wipe some or most of it off; spray with Dullcote; and so on. Although the process is slow and painstaking, it is remarkably satisfying work and very different to the creative blur of airbrush weathering.*

24: *Now we have some pronounced streaks running down from where sooty deposits collect in the roof panels. I used a fine-pointed No 1 brush for this, whereas I did most of the gouache-weathering work with a round-tipped No 3.*

25: *A pause for reflection: I'm well satisfied with the bodysides but the roof is still rather flat . . .*

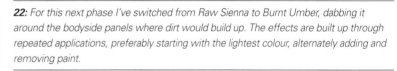

26: . . . which calls for a few dabs of black weathering powder on the cab roof, mixed with soot from the domestic hearth, to simulate spillage of coal fines when passing through loading bunkers . . .

27: . . . and a shiny patch behind the roof fans, clearly visible in high-angle photographs, which serves to emphasise the sootiness around the exhausts for which a further coat of unpolished Metalcote Gunmetal is needed.

28: When 56075 was repainted from red-stripe to triple-grey Railfreight, the West Yorkshire Enterprise nameplates were repositioned. Eventually witness lines began to appear on the bodysides, marking the former fixing points. Having marked their position in pencil at 3mm intervals, I represented these by spots of Burnt Umber gouache applied with a No 0 brush.

29: You often see swipe marks in the bodyside dirt, where the locomotive has brushed against foliage and other lineside obstructions. I add these by gentle scraping with a blunt craft knife, just sufficient to carve lines through the gouache weathering but not enough to break through into the plastic.

30 The addition of numbers, plates and plaques – all from the excellent Extreme Etchings range – seems almost an afterthought, scarcely impacting on the overall effect. And there we have it – a workhorse of the coalfields, as typical of its working environment as the grubby 2-8-0s of half a century ago . . .